WORKING FROM HOME IS YOUR SUPERPOWER

Working remotely?

Juggling videoconferences, emails, children,
and interruptions requires new skills.

When you finish this book, you'll have
Working from Home Super-Skills!

Also by Janis Allen

Manage Your Time Like It's All You've Got—It Is!
(with Shauna Costello & Allison King)

*From Boo-Hiss to Bravo: Behavior-Based Scorecards People Will Use
and Like* (with Allison King)

Performance Teams: Creating the Feedback Loop

*I Saw What You Did & I Know Who You Are: Bloopers, Blunders, & Successes
in Giving and Receiving Recognition* (with Gail Snyder)

You Made My Day: Creating Co-Worker Recognition & Relationships
(with Michael McCarthy)

Team Up!

*How to Engage, Involve and Motivate Employees:
Building a Culture of Lean Leadership and Two-Way Communication*
(with Michael McCarthy)

*Ready? Set? Engage! Field Guide for Employees to Create Their Own Culture
of Participation and Implement Innovative Ideas* (with Michael McCarthy)

Stories from a Sandy Mush Girl

"We Shall Come Home Victorious." Stories of WWII Veterans

Also by Michael McCarthy

Sustain Your Gains: The People Side of Lean-Six Sigma

You Made My Day: Creating Co-Worker Recognition & Relationships
(with Janis Allen)

How to Engage, Involve and Motivate Employees:
Building a Culture of Lean Leadership and Two-Way Communication
(with Janis Allen)

Ready? Set? Engage! Field Guide for Employees to Create Their Own
Culture of Participation and Implement Innovative Ideas (with Janis Allen)

Also by Gail Snyder

Removing Obstacles to Safety: A Behavior-Based Approach (with Judy Agnew)

I Saw What You Did & I Know Who You Are: Bloopers, Blunders, & Successes in Giving and Receiving Recognition (with Janis Allen)

Books Edited

Sustain Your Gains: The People Side of Lean-Six Sigma

You Can't Apologize to a Dawg: A Down-Home Guide to Leadership

Working from Home
Is Your SuperPower

Your Guide to Working Remotely

Janis Allen

Michael McCarthy

Gail Snyder

Castletownbere Press

Working from Home is Your SuperPower
Your Guide to Working Remotely

ISBN 9798717773560

Printed by KDP in the United States of America

Castletownbere Press

Cover Design: Advertising PLUS
Lawrenceville, Georgia / adplus@mac.com

Line Illustrations: Laurie Allen Klein
The Curious Pangolin, Orlando, Florida

This book is for sale on Amazon.com

For information on corporate and volume discounts, please email
janisallen@janisallen.com

DEDICATION

I dedicate this book to Jack Joyner, my friend since college
who generously shared tips gleaned from 12 years of working remotely.

~ Michael McCarthy

I dedicate this book to Michel Johns Robertson, who for 15 years has offered
creative ideas, candid feedback, and loving support of my writing projects.
Her expert eye for text and design makes everything better.

~ Janis Allen

I dedicate this book to my husband, Jack Snyder, who has patiently (most of
the time) listened to my working-from-home woes and adventures.

~ Gail Snyder

IN APPRECIATION

to these successful working-from-home professionals who contributed their unique, memorable, and clever ideas for this book.

Harry Halmshaw
University professor teaching English to South Korean students
from home office via videoconferencing and recorded videos

Stephen Jackson
Home Designer creating construction drawings for new houses and
additions/renovations for 24 years, working from his home office for 16
years

Jack Joyner
Consulting IT specialist working remotely for IBM, serving international
customers at all hours of the day and night for a dozen years

Russell Justice
Founding Partner, The Transformation Network; Senior Technical Associate
in Management Engineering Services for Eastman Chemical's worldwide
applications of Applied Behavior Analysis

Dr. Lori Ludwig
Founder of Performance Blueprints, dedicated to behavioral systems analysis
to optimize the impact of organizations, working from home for 11 years

Greg Maag
Principal, Conley Rose Law Firm specializing in intellectual property, who,
with his firm's 100 employees, works and manages his team
mostly from home

Shawn McCarthy
University professor teaching English to South Korean students both in-person and from home via videoconferencing and recorded videos

Kathy Peterson
Owner of Advertising Plus Graphic Design, working from home to design marketing and business materials for 30 years

Eric Rasheed
Dad of football player, UPS delivery driver for 31 years

Michel Robertson
Owner of Accountability Business Services and board member of three non-profits, working partially from home for 5 years

Brenda Smith
Corporate HR Payroll Specialist for a Fortune Global 500 company

CONTENTS

Preface..xiii

Introduction: WORKING FROM HOME Challenges & Chuckles...................xvii

SECTION ONE: CLAIM & SET UP YOUR WORKSPACE..........................1

    1. Claim Your Workspace...3
    2. Signage: Mark Your Territory...................................9
    3. What Does It Take to Keep You In Your Workspace?...................15
    4. Don't Touch My Stuff: The Joy of Office Supplies.......................19
    5. Declutter...23

SECTION TWO: WHAT YOU DO INSIDE YOUR WORKSPACE.....................27

    PART ONE: Organizing the Way You Do Your Work.....................29
    6. Organizing Your Workflow......................................31
    7. Setting Up Your Schedule.......................................37
    8. "Mommy, Where Do Deadlines Come From?"....................41
    9. Listen to Your Body Clock.......................................49
    10. Found Time...55

    PART TWO: Communications...59
    11. Email: Needles, Not Haystacks.................................61
    12. Phone Calls: Chatty or Concise?...............................71
    13. Death by Meeting?..77

    PART THREE: Your Work Habits.......................................85
    14. Procrastinate Your Procrastinating.............................87
    15. Weed Out Your Time Wasters...................................99
    16. Let Go...105
    17. Let's Make a Deal..109

PART FOUR: Your Work Relationships.................................115
   18. Work Remotely Without Becoming Remote.............117
   19. Water-Cooler Time....................................123
   20. Make Friends with Your Delivery Drivers............129

PART FIVE: Sharpen the Saw--You!..........................131
   21. Exercise. Give Your Brain a Break and a Boost......133
   22. Sleep...143
   23. Power Napping.......................................147

SECTION THREE: DEFENDING YOUR WORKSPACE AGAINST INVADERS.............153

   24. "THEY KNOW I'M HERE!"...............................155
   25. Passport Entry.....................................161
   26. Interrupt Interruptions: Yes You Can..............169
   27. Dr. No Is Your Friend.............................177
   28. "And Stay Out!"...................................181
   29. Guard Your Time Like It's All You've Got. It Is!...189

How We Used the Tips in This Book to Write This Book..........193
FAQs..197
Share Your Tips & Tribulations................................199
About the Authors...201
Recommended Resources...205
Index...209

PREFACE

We wrote this book for people who

A. Work Remotely

1. You'll learn how to assertively manage your time and space.
2. You'll get tips on planning your work and working your plan.
3. You'll get tips that keep you focused, help you work successfully, and keep your career on track.

B. Operate a Home-Based Business

1. You'll learn how to set and meet your goals.
2. You'll learn how to focus on doing the things you are good at, while getting help with other necessary tasks.
3. You'll learn how to get the professional contact and stimulation of ideas to keep your business vibrant.

Observations on Working Remotely from an Employer's Perspective

Here are insights from Greg Maag, principal of a large law firm, on changes from the previous pattern of working in the office.

1. Challenges to business effectiveness and professional growth

- *The skill of "reading the audience" and pivoting or adapting accordingly will be hard to learn with everyone remote from each other.*

- *There are no casual get-togethers in a small conference room or kitchen as before. Those were extremely valuable in sharing information and teaching the firm's culture; this is to the detriment of training younger professionals.*

2. Work/Personal Time

- *Breaks can be quick chores or errands that would otherwise be put off to the weekend. Many home chores are very relaxing for me, so these breaks are nice ways to be totally rid of work pressures at times.*

- *People are spreading out work tasks and emailing up to 10:00 or 11:00 in the evening. We're all more attentive to checking emails outside of "normal" work hours—not so much that something is imperative, but to keep the information flowing and allow the email sender to complete a task on his/her chosen schedule.*

- *Where both parents are now working from home and keeping their kids educated through online learning, it seems impossible. How do single parents manage? The job has to suffer.*

Observations on the Home-Based Business

Dr. Lori Ludwig, observes:

I have worked from home for the past 11 years and love the freedom and flexibility. What I love:

- *Uninterrupted focus time*
- *Taking care of household tasks during work breaks*
- *Work from anywhere in the world*

Whether Working Remotely or Home-based Business

This book will give you tips to shorten your workdays, create a personal workspace, streamline your work processes, make meetings more productive, fight off interruptions, and manage your time for a work/life balance you will like.

It's a wonderful world we live in—where we are able to work from home. Let's make the most of it, productively and enjoyably!

~ Janis Allen

 # INTRODUCTION: WORKING FROM HOME CHALLENGES & CHUCKLES

Working from home is a new challenge for many.

Your co-authors Gail, Mike, and Janis decided to write a book about working from home while . . . working from home! We are corporate trainers, business writers, and curriculum designers. We know that *what you laugh at, you remember.* So, we decided to present some serious stuff spiced with humor. You may have challenges, but we'll help you make them humorous challenges.

> **What you laugh at, you remember.**

Laugh and learn is our motto. We poke fun at the foibles and fantasies of working from home. We make the serious stuff FUN.

The Great A-Sleepening of 2020

When many workers began working remotely in 2020, a great awakening occurred. Actually, it was a great a-sleepening—the discovery that when I work from home, *I can sleep in later!*

> **When I work from home, I can sleep in later!**

Because I have zero commute time. What's not to like?

Just as much work is getting done at home.

A large company's VP had an Archimedes "Eureka" moment: *Just as much work got done at home as at the office!*

She jubilantly explained this to her CEO. "So, what are we paying office rent for? And office phone lines? And that awful, powdered creamer for coffee? And K-cup machines? We spend a fortune on K-cups!"

More distractions when working from home?

With roommates, children, spouses, pizza deliveries, daytime TV, text notifications, your children's Legos and the refrigerator, it's easy to get distracted. When distractions take a bite out of your workday, you end up working longer hours to get the job done.

My co-author Gail writes: "Distractions can be abundant. One day, for example, while getting my mail, my neighbor drove up on his ATV and asked, 'Want to go to a garage sale?' I did; purchased a roll of wallpaper border that I never used. I admit that distraction was on me."

A New Nemesis

And then we discovered a new nemesis for Work From Homers: the evil **Dr. Zoom**. Motto: *Record video when I see your*

Meet the evil Dr. Zoom. Motto: Record video when I see your plaid pajamas!

---

plaid pajamas. Dr. Zoom can embarrass you if you forget to activate your super-protective no-video button or no-audio button. Who knows how much of you he has already seen? And your little dog too!

Working from Home—Three Steps

- First, you decide where your workspace will be. You look at several locations with features you want: napping couch, cable TV, mini-bar, etc.
- Second, you learn how to work within your workspace effectively, utilizing laptop, Pandora, videoconferencing, Pez dispensers, etc.
- Third, you learn how to defend your workspace and worktime from distractions: dogs, cats, boa constrictors, spouse, tugging toddlers, etc.

So, there are three sections to this book:

1. CLAIM & SET UP YOUR WORKSPACE
2. WHAT YOU DO INSIDE YOUR WORKSPACE
3. DEFENDING YOUR WORKSPACE AGAINST INVADERS

So, don't stress over the challenges. Laugh at them instead. As Jimmy Buffett sang, "If we couldn't laugh, we would all go insane." ~ *Changes in Latitudes, Changes In Attitudes*

We invite you to Work from Home with us as we reveal to you secret WFH SuperPowers you didn't even know you had. All for one low price cheaper than a home-meal delivery from Uber-Eats.

~ Mike McCarthy

1. Claim & Set Up Your WorkSpace

2. What You Do Inside Your Workspace

3. Defending Your Workspace Against Invaders

Where are you on this map?

Happy with your workspace set-up? Go to 2.

Happy with the way you do your work? Go to 3.

Good at defending your time & space? Put down this book.

Just kidding! We can make you EVEN BETTER.

Start here!

SECTION ONE:

CLAIM & SET UP YOUR WORKSPACE

A GOOD CRAFTSMAN NEEDS GOOD TOOLS.

SET UP A GOOD WORKSPACE WITH GOOD TOOLS.

1. Claim Your Workspace

Mike writes: Yours. Yours only. **All yours**. You need a workspace that is YOURS and YOURS ONLY. Yes, you read that right. ALL CAPS. I'M RAISING MY VOICE FOR EMPHASIS! Stake out a place, room, or corner for your workspace. You need dedicated workspace. Why?

- For your sanity
- For saving time (You won't have to go looking for your stuff. It's all right here.)
- For a focused space where everything says "Here's the next thing to do," and "This space is here to help you get work done."

Where is Your Workspace? Stake Your Claim.

I'm here to help you do your work!

Stake a claim: declare your right to something. This expression refers to the practice of putting stakes around the perimeter of a piece of land to which an ownership claim is laid. It's American in origin, dating from the California gold rush of 1849, when the prospectors registered their claims to individual plots of land with stakes.

To get the gold (your valuable nuggets of work accomplished), you too have to stake your claim to a workspace. Let's go prospecting in your house or apartment. You're looking for a spot where you can

- **Place** your papers, tools or laptop on a flat surface
- **Plug** in a lamp, tools and charge cords for phone and computer
- **Remain** during work hours without having to move aside for other people to use the space

We heard about one person who had only an ironing board for a desk, so we consider ourselves lucky to at least have a firm surface to work on.

Spare bedroom, kitchen table, dining room, family room, basement, corner of your bedroom? Found it? Now let's set it up for success. Whose success? Yours, of course!

Design & Set Up Your Workspace

Congratulations! You are now a workspace designer. Just as interior designers coordinate colors, you're coordinating the elements of work flow. An interior designer will tell you, "These colors clash. Get rid of them." You will tell yourself, "This item distracts me from my work. I'll get rid of it."

My co-author, freelance editor and writer (and long-time WFH veteran) Gail Snyder tells the story of how behavioral scientist and author B. F. Skinner organized his desktop. No, not a computer desktop, because there were no desktop computers in his day. An actual, physical, wooden desktop. He placed all the reference books he might use on his desk within arm's reach. Why? He said that he knew that if he had to get up from his chair and find the book on a bookshelf, he might not make the effort.

In the world of behavior analysis, having to get up out of your chair to find a book is called response cost. It "costs" too much time and effort to do it. Result? For Skinner, an important reference for his book or article would be skipped over.

This was an early example of what the Lean world now calls *5S*. Lean principles to make work flow more easily (derived from the Toyota Production System) are now used in IT software development, insurance, and publishing. They can be applied to any work process. For more on Lean principles, see my book *Sustain Your Gains*, available at www.the5Sstore.com/sustainyourgains.

What are the items you use in your daily work at home? This may include a computer, cell phone, copier, printer, scanner, and perhaps a microphone for

Move any item used daily to within arm's reach.

Zoom calls. Possibly a notepad and pen. To set yourself up for success, place these items within easy arm's reach. Oh, and a coffee cup. Don't forget the coffee cup!

Let's do a quick check. In the space below, list some items you use as part of your daily work in the left-hand column. In the right-hand column, check off whether each is within arm's reach.

Items I use daily	Within arm's reach?

The goal of 5S is to make your work simpler and easier to do. If you have to frequently go to another room to get pages out of your printer, for example, move the printer to the same room. Preferably next to you.

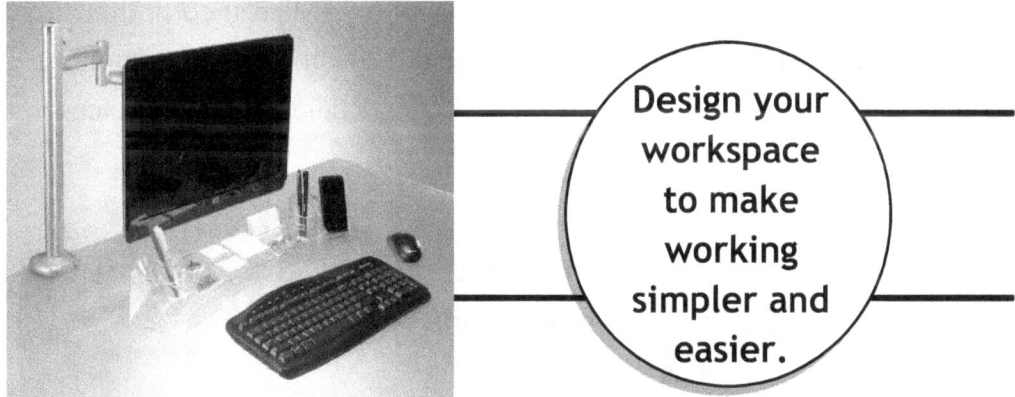

Design your workspace to make working simpler and easier.

What if you have to share your workspace? Like using the dining room table which periodically has to be used for . . . dining? You might try our patented "**Office in a Box**™" technique.

Put everything you need in a box or plastic tub: notepad, pens, laptop, power cords, mouse, external hard drive, etc.

- Store your portable office in a box in a place where curious children and lazy roommates are unlikely to disturb or move it ("I need a pen, so I'll take John's office box to my bedroom desk to search for one." And forget to return it, so John spends 45 minutes looking for it.)
- When it's time to work, take the box to your shared workspace and unload what you need to get started.
- When you're finished work for the day, pack the box and hide it away from others. See chapter 4, "Don't Touch My Stuff: The Joy of Office Supplies!"

For a shining example, look at these pictures of my (Mike's) computer tub. It is actually a Rubbermaid food storage box, so it has the added advantage of a sealed lid for liquid-proofing my laptop against spilled coffee or juice.

< LEFT:
Office in a box at work scene

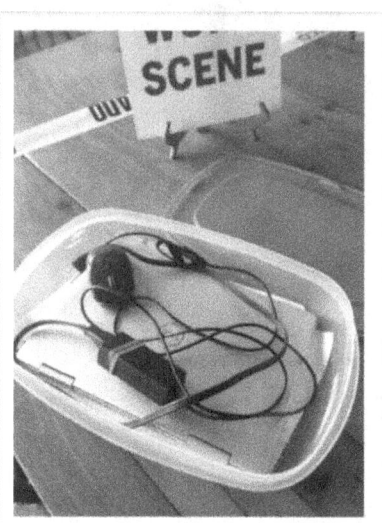

> RIGHT:
Inside: mouse, power cord, laptop

Once upon a time I did spill coffee on my laptop. Coffee on a keyboard makes a distinctive *snap-crackle-pop* sizzle to inform you that your laptop is fried. If you want a beverage next to your laptop, put the cup inside a saucer or bowl. Like the levees in New Orleans, it will hold back the flood of slopped coffee from your laptop.

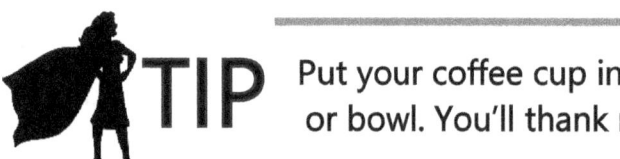

TIP Put your coffee cup in a saucer or bowl. You'll thank me later.

2. Signage:

Mark Your Territory

Mike writes: Our kitchen is a one-person kitchen. When I'm cooking breakfast, I don't want Janis in there. Why? Because we end up bumping into each other (and maybe spilling from the pots in our hands). So the rule is—when I'm cooking, stay out!

This is a good rule for your workspace. When others intrude, stuff gets moved, butts get bumped, you get distracted and it takes extra time and effort to get your work done. This applies even when you have to claim part of a common area as your workspace, like the dining room table. You may have to vacate the table at suppertime, but during your working hours it needs to be yours and yours alone.

How can you politely but firmly remind others in your household to stay out of your workspace?

Signage. Since this room is not normally segregated for a workspace, it's helpful if you have a visual signal that now it IS a workspace. This saves a lot of nagging and annoyance. "I told you, Mom is working in here!" "Jay, I thought we agreed that after 8:00 AM, the bedroom is off-limits because then it's a workspace!"

Maybe it's a "sometimes workspace," like the kitchen table. Sometimes we eat there; sometimes I work there. Naturally, children, spouses, and roommates can get confused about when they're allowed to use it.

Signs Can Work Wonders

Here's a scientific case study published in the *Journal of Scientific Spousal Negotiative Entanglement Psychology*. Published whenever there is a kerfuffle at our house.

The Case of the Nibbled Nuggets. I am a fast eater. I am also a vacuum eater. Like a vacuum cleaner, I suck up all particles of food within a three-foot radius of wherever I am. My wife and business partner Janis is a slow eater. There are plates of petrified scrambled eggs from the 1970s in her office. Our next business venture is to start a museum of fossilized foods. What happens when Mike the Food Vacuum finds these tidbits? You guessed it! They're gone!

What happens when the Slow Eater discovers that her fossilizing omelet has disappeared? Let's just say it's not a pretty sight.

Our solution? Signage. Now, when Janis sets aside a plate of food for possible consumption in 2055, she "marks her territory" with this sign.

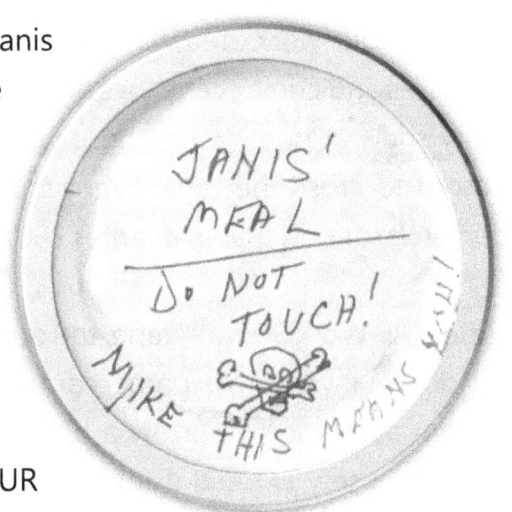

This sign automatically flips the "off" switch on my galloping gullet and saves the marriage. Diligent readers will ask, "What has that got to do with my workspace?" Answer: MARK YOUR WORKSPACE with SIGNAGE.

Fun with Work Scene™ Tape

Ever watch crime shows? Of course, you do! Usually when you are procrastinating (see chapter 14 for tips on how to procrastinate your urge to procrastinate).

How do the CSI, FBI, and SAT (Special Agents of Television) keep random spectators and clue thieves away from the crime scene? You know this one. Crime scene tape! Bright yellow and black tape wound around the place.

One easy signage/territory marker solution is **Work Scene**™ tape for your workspace. PUBLISHERS WARNING LABEL: If your workspace includes a couch, *don't' take naps inside your tape.* Someone may mistake you for a dead body and call CSI!

Rope off your work area with **Work Scene**™ tape. In police shows, only the detectives and crime scene investigators are allowed to cross the tape. In your reality show at home, only those with the proper badges and passports are allowed to cross the tape. Who issues the badges and passports? You of course! (More on that in chapter 25.)

Inside your **Work Scene**™ tape, the only items allowed are the things that help you do your work. No game controllers. No magazines. No popcorn. No children intruding to borrow a pen. If a pen is inside the tape, it should be there because you need it for your work. Therefore, it's off-limits to anyone but you.

How to mark your territory:

- Rope it off with yellow flagging tape.
- Mark the boundaries with orange cones.
- Placard it with a "WORK SCENE" or "WORK ZONE" sign.

Co-author Janis Allen working safely inside protective **Work Scene**™ tape.

Gail writes: As empty nesters, we don't really need signs, but that doesn't stop me. One of my workspace signs reads, "Beware of . . . Well . . . Just Beware." I also have a brightly painted fan blade pointing toward me printed with the word "Psychopath." That should keep workspace invaders away!

Post a sign. Then growl
if anyone gets too close.

3. What Does It Take to Keep You in Your Workspace?

Janis writes: What does it take to keep you in your workspace, not wandering around your house getting a ton of notworking done? Let's face it, without a boss or co-worker peer pressure to stay focused on work, it's tempting to lollygag and dawdle. Or as one colleague, a good Southerner, taught us to say, "I'm fixin' to do something. I reckon I'll do something. Actually, I'm just fixin' to reckon."

Getting a ton of notworking done?

We asked Kathy Peterson, owner of Advertising Plus, what it takes to keep her motivated. Her answer: "Money! When I have a project to work on, it becomes a priority over any household-type work." That says it for us, too!

Here's what it takes to keep me in my workspace:

1. **The right chair.** For about 10 years, I used an office chair I picked up at a yard sale. Not for sale but pushed out near the sidewalk with a FREE sign on it. It was just fine except for the rip in the fake Naugahyde armrest. (Just a note about fake Naugahyde. Naugahyde is fake leather. When you have fake Naugahyde, that's really tacky.) But duct tape covered that rip just fine. I put a lower-back support thing in because my back never touched the chair, but the elastic bands kept popping and the back support ended up underneath me (ouch).

   I finally found a much nicer desk chair at another yard sale for $10.00. Our town has a donation center that will take anything, so I loaded up the fake Naugahyde chair to take it in. Mike (who regularly goes through my trash to make sure I'm not throwing any "good stuff" away) saw the chair in my car trunk and rescued it. I don't know where it is today.

   But my newer, ten-dollar chair adjusts to the perfect "booster seat" height for my 5'1" tallness. With the 'fits over' back support pictured at right ($7 plus shipping), it provides an inviting and comfortable place to perch for as long as my brain keeps producing.

   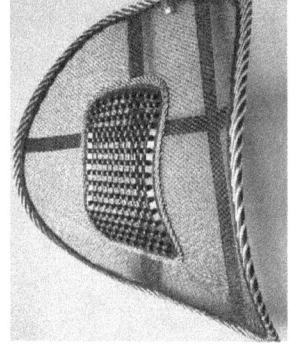

Treat yourself to a comfortable but firmly supportive piece of furniture for sitting. IT consultant Jack Joyner reminds us, "You may spend up to one-third of your work week sitting in that chair." Scary!

2. **The right temperature**. Mine: toasty warm in winter, "ceiling fan" breezy in summer. If your taste in climate is different from other family members', get a box fan or space heater. A sweater or scarf is always dangling on the back of my chair.

3. **The right light**. Joyner advises, "Don't use overhead lighting in your office. Carefully placed lamps will reduce screen glare and eye strain." Also, invest in shades or curtains if needed to reduce glare to make your eyes comfortable. At different times of day and angles of the sun, get up and stretch your back and shoulders while you open or close your solar shades or diffusers.

4. **Cocoon**. Treat yourself to accessories that make your workspace pleasant and inviting. These will entice you to stay in your space and be productive. A scented candle? Angling your chair toward a window for an outdoor view while you're thinking? Soft background music?

5. **A privacy screen** can simulate a closed door, sort of. Most can be folded and stored when you're using your dining room for actual dining. In 2021, furniture company *The Inside* reported 150% growth in folding screens over the previous year. Prices for screens start under $50.00. Even if they aren't impervious to intrusions, they can screen your view from distractions of all the chores you

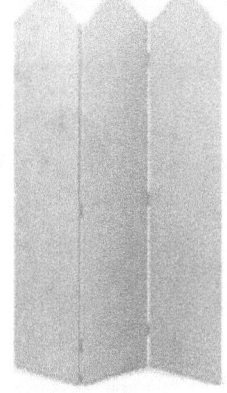

could be doing in your house while you procrastinate that work project you don't want to tackle.

Bonus: when it's quittin' time, you can make a dramatic entrance into the family space by strutting out from behind your screen (or out of your office) and loudly announcing, "Hi, Honey, I'm home!" This clever idea is from Karen Adamedes in her book, *Professional in Pajamas*.

6. **Post your office hours** humorously. This gives you a visual to point to when reminding your family members that you're working right now. Here are some fun examples.

*More on the use of passports in Chapter 25

Dad's Office Hours

8:00 – 12:00 & 1:00 – 5:00

Interruptions allowed at:

_10:15_

if you have a valid passport*

TIP

Make your workspace a magnet that pulls you in.

4. Don't Touch My Stuff: The Joy of Office Supplies

Janis writes: I love office supplies in the same way I loved school supplies a few decades ago. Almost as much as I love lists. Working from home, we each get to assemble the items that will warmly welcome us to our world of work every day. No pesky office mates sneaking into our cubicles to "borrow" a never-to-be-returned favorite pen.

What are the things that can give you a comfortable, positive feeling when you enter your workspace? Perhaps:

- A neat desktop with spaces between each separate document (no overlapping allowed), waiting patiently overnight for your return (Do documents sleep?)

- Pens and pencils leaning casually but with perfect posture in their attractive pencil cup, jar, or "memento" coffee mug, ready for action. I only have gel pens (blue, red, and green) because I like the way gel flows without scratchiness.

- A fully charged laptop, packed with priceless files and ready for travel (if only to the next room)

- The perfect mouse that snuggles into your palm. Have you named your mouse? My mouse, Minnie, has a rollerball and is large; looks more like a hedgehog.

- 3" X 5" pad for my <u>daily</u> to-do list. I use this small size to prevent me from writing 15 items (way too many to complete in one day).

  If your to-do list is for your whole week's work or your whole life's work, it might be a tad larger.

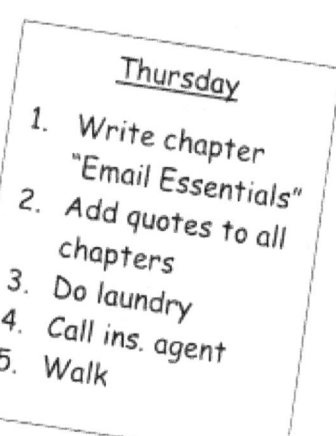

Thursday
1. Write chapter "Email Essentials"
2. Add quotes to all chapters
3. Do laundry
4. Call ins. agent
5. Walk

Thursday
1. Write chapter "Email Essentials"
2. Add quotes to all chapters
3. Do laundry
4. Call ins. agent
5. Walk
CELEBRATE!

I limit my list to my <u>daily</u> goals because I love to get those suckers all checked off. Then I ball up the list and confidently dunk it in the trashcan the same way I shot lay-ups for my seventh-grade basketball team, the Alexander Elementary School Blue Devils.

I mix personal tasks with business tasks on my daily to-do list. Taking a break from work to do a household chore is refreshing to me. It's one more item I get to check off my list. What a cheap date!

- Legal pad with stiff cardboard backing for taking notes during meetings. The stiff backing helps when I want to get away from my desk and sit on the porch with the pad on my lap. A change of scenery is refreshing and gets me walking around.

The pad also serves as a good "backing" when I want to grab a printed page out of the printer and place it on top of the pad for editing with a red pen. I catch errors on the printed page that I don't catch on my screen, so my trashcan sometimes fills up with first, second, third, and fourth drafts.

Document-Sized Shelves

Inexpensive desktop shelves for papers and files are my old friends. I'm a writer and always have actual books and papers in my work area for reference.

I'm usually working on two or three projects at a time, so I use these plastic shelves to keep papers or books for each project together, and get them "out of the way" when working on something different. Plastic, metal, wood: treat yourself and enjoy the neat physical appearance of your desk or work area to make you feel organized!

At right is a photo of my shelves. I like seeing an empty shelf. Makes me feel caught up and in control.

But Don't Touch My Stuff! I want everything to be in the same place I left it when I walk back into my work area. That also helps me feel in control, and saves searching time.

What are the office supplies or accessories that spark joy for you? Think of how much time you spend in your work area. Treat yourself to things that make your work easier and more pleasant. You're worth it!

 **TIP**   Choose office supplies that make your work easier.

5. Declutter

Mike writes: In chapter one, we talked about the industry technique called "5S"—simplifying your workspace to make it easier to do your work. That includes removing everything that is <u>not needed</u> for your work.

Why? Two reasons:

1. When there's a clutter of objects, it takes more time to dig and search for the one you need for your work. This is wasted time that you could use to get work done and then have free time for you and your family.

    For example: Find the screwdriver you need in this drawer. →

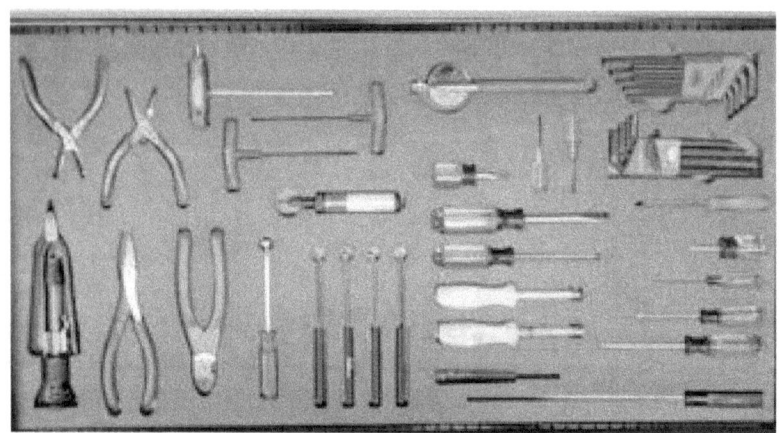

Now look in this drawer.
See what I mean?

←

2. When there's a clutter of objects, each one might remind you of some other <u>non-work</u> thing to do. If you begin doing these other things, you aren't doing your job. If you even *think* about these other things, it takes time away from thinking about how to do your work projects.

When your desktop contains ONLY what you need to do your work, you are not distracted. You find what you need to get started easily and quickly. (Like coffee!)

**De-clutter your desk.
Clutter distracts you.**

Gail writes: My desk must be uncluttered, one project folder at a time on the desktop. However, since I work alone, I do have toys: a squeezable stress releasor—mine is a Minion, a Halloween monkey that says funny things when squeezed: "I want candy, candy, candy in my handy, handy, handy." I also have one of those repeating toys for kids. Mine is a hamster. He repeats phrases that you

**One project folder at
a time on the desktop**

say to him. I might pick him up and say, "Wow, you did a great job on that article." He then repeats it back to me in a hamster voice. Sad, but true! (Got to get kudos somehow!)

The de-clutter concept applies to your computer screen too. How long would it take to find your document on the screen below?

And on this screen below? Place a single shortcut icon for your current project on your desktop screen. File all others under "documents."

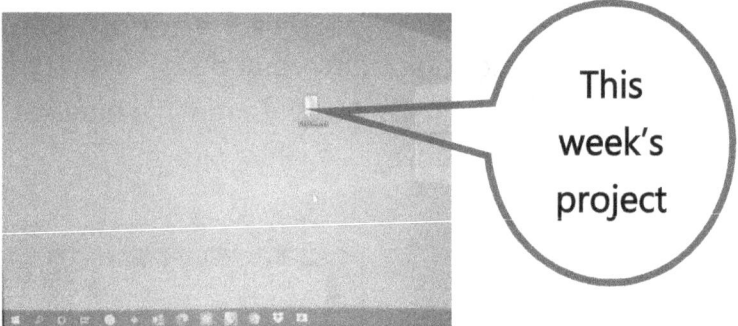

This week's project

A tip from contributor Michel Robertson: place the document to begin tomorrow morning's work in the center of your desk just before you stop working for the day.

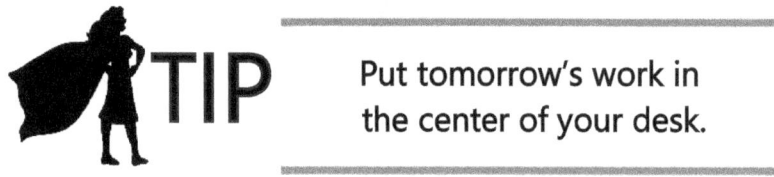

TIP

Put tomorrow's work in the center of your desk.

SECTION TWO:
WHAT YOU DO INSIDE YOUR WORKSPACE

PART ONE:
ORGANIZING THE WAY
YOU DO YOUR WORK

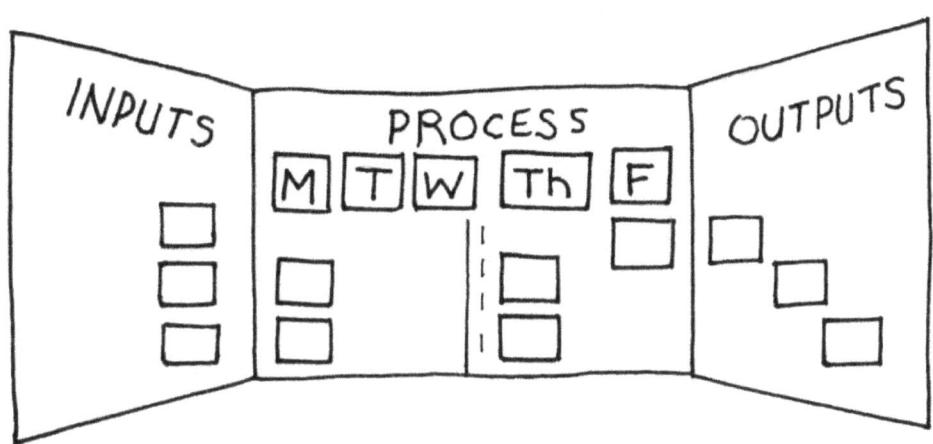

 6. Organizing Your Workflow

Mike writes: What is workflow and what does it have to do with working from home? Ever seen a sink full of dirty dishes? Shucks, it happens to the best of us. What problem does this create for you? That's right; no plate to eat from. Like a stopped-up sink drain, your dish workflow has

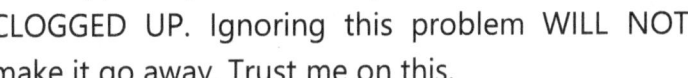

CLOGGED UP. Ignoring this problem WILL NOT make it go away. Trust me on this.

Once upon a time in a bachelor galaxy far, far away, I had two roommates. I'll call them Fred and Louie. By luck of the draw, Fred liked to cook! Louie and I looked at each other and rejoiced. It was a miracle

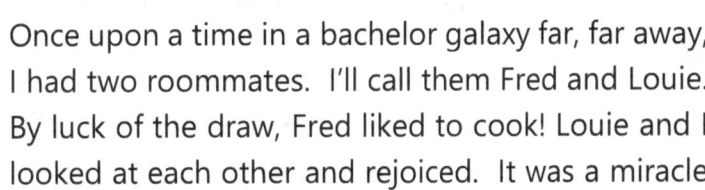

unheard of in the legends and histories of roommates.

Fred said, "If I do the cooking, then you two guys wash the dishes, right?" Louie and I nodded gratefully.

Louie and I agreed to take turns washing the dishes each night. First, it was my turn. Then it was Louie's turn. Then it was . . . wait, Louie didn't take his turn. I did the dishes. Then it was my turn. Then it was Louie's turn . . . but . . . Fred even did the dishes a time or two.

Then the Rebel Alliance was forged: Fred and I decided not to wash the dishes until Louie took his turn. The dishes piled up. The pots and pans sat in dirty grey dish water. With no clean pots to cook with, we ate food from fast-food, take-out bags.

Weeks passed. The dishes sat in the sink until, one day, I noticed something

green growing over the edge of the sink. Like a low-budget horror film, it was the **Green Creature from the Sink of the Unwashed**! To save us from a horror-film fate, the three of us became Jedi Dishwashers. Order was restored in the bachelor galaxy.

What do dirty dishes have to do with workflow?

The sink full of dirty dishes was a stoppage in the kitchen workflow sequence: use dishes -> wash dishes -> return dishes to shelf -> use dishes again. Like a traffic jam, everything stopped. In the sink.

Whether you work from home or work from a (shudder!) cubicle, an established workflow routine will help you in several ways:

1. The diagram below shows you a basic IPO flow: INPUTS (work assignments, information & materials) -> PROCESS (what you do to get the job done) -> OUTPUTS (your finished work)

2. When you match your weekly calendar with the estimated time to do the work process for each input, you can plan realistic deadlines/target dates/finish-line dates for your projects. In this example, 3 projects are on the INPUT side. Estimated time for all 3 = 5 days, so you can get them done in your PROCESS 5-day workweek. On Friday, you should be able to show the 3 projects as completed OUTPUTS.

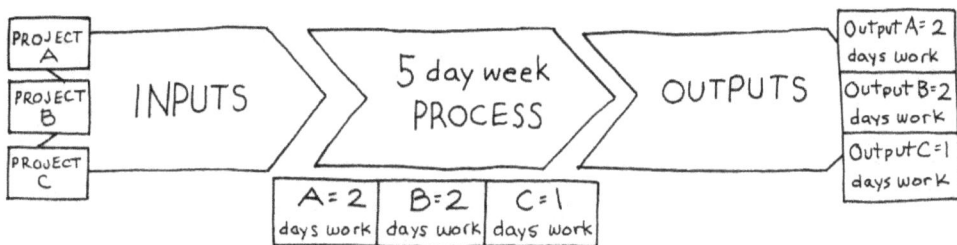

3. When you see your IPO flow, you can spot potential stoppages/overloads. Too much work for the available time = deadline won't be met. Plan your workflow, or your work will OVERFLOW and you'll have to work overtime to catch up.

4. When you see that your workweek is filled, it is time to ask, "Which project do you want me to delay?" Otherwise, <u>all</u> your projects may be delayed. MAJOR WORK CLOG ALERT! Time to re-negotiate and re-plan your workload with your boss or customer.

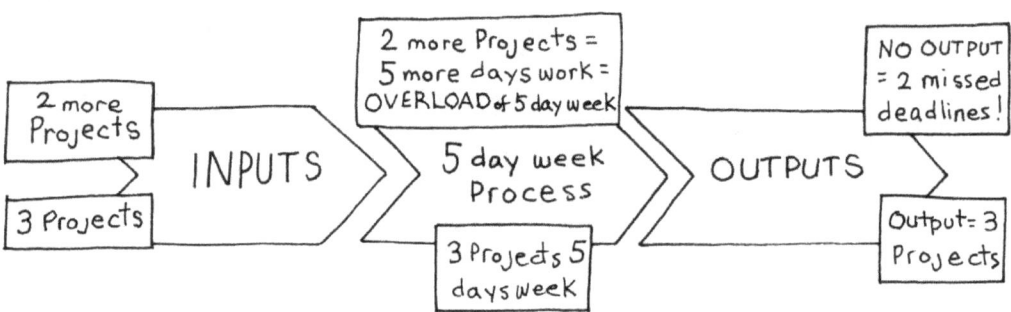

You can make your own IPO chart with file folders and small sticky notes. Just staple or tape two file folders together. With a Sharpie marker, label left to right INPUTS, PROCESS, OUTPUTS. Subdivide the middle PROCESS section into the 5 days of your workweek. Estimate the number of hours or days it will take to do the work of each input. Mark those days or hours on your PROCESS

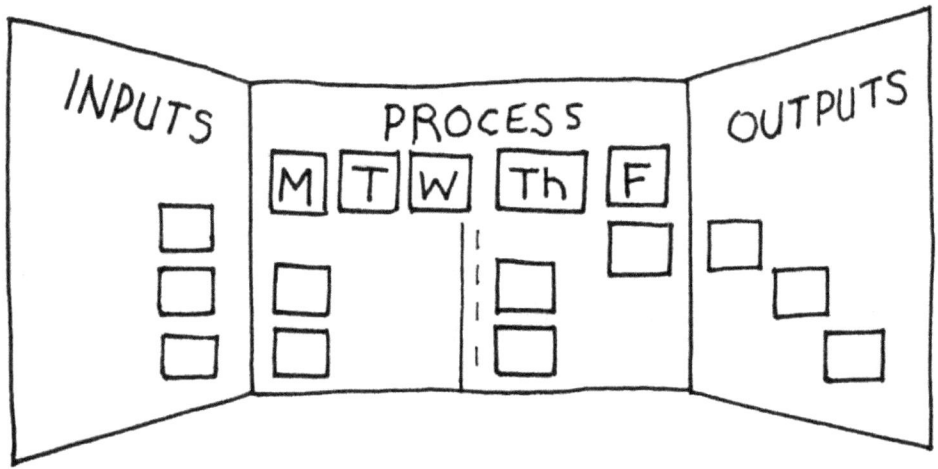

Monday—Friday. When each project is completed, place a sticky note on the OUTPUTS side to show completion.

I recommend propping up this IPO chart (or posting on a bulletin board) in front of you so that you can see it at all times:

- What work is coming in: (INPUTS)
- How much of your work week is committed to the work: (PROCESS)
- When the finished work is done: (OUTPUTS)

If it is on a computer screen, it will get buried and forgotten 6 screens in. Propping it in front of you keeps it simple and *always visible,* just like dirty dishes in sink (INPUTS), wash dishes (PROCESS), clean dishes drying in dishrack (OUTPUTS).

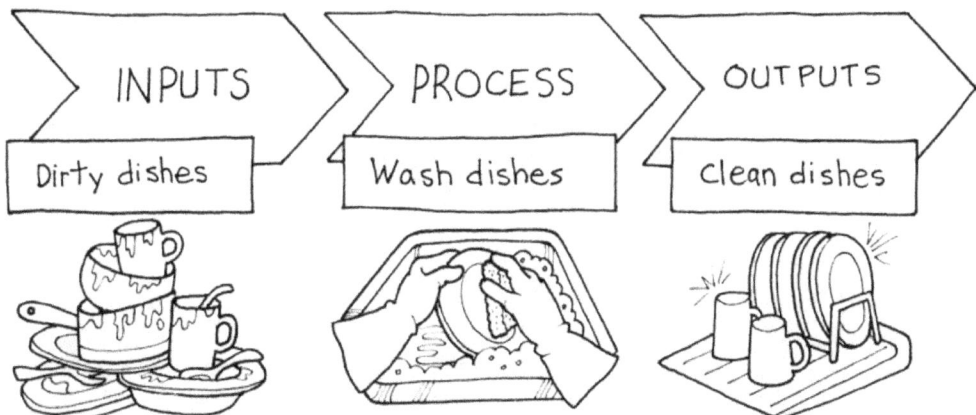

Take two file folders or cardboard and make an IPO chart for yourself. From your scheduled work this week, pick a short project and name it on a sticky note. Put it on the INPUT side of your chart. Estimate the hours it will take to complete this project. Place multiple sticky notes that add up to enough hours on various days M-F on the PROCESS section in the middle.

Now you have begun to make your workflow visible. Out of sight = out of mind. In sight = in control. Whose control? Yours.

Out of sight = out of mind.
In sight = in control.

7. Setting Up Your Schedule

Mike writes: When to work on what? Set up your own schedule, or, by default, your time will be filled by others. For this week, you have your IPO chart described in chapter 6.

For projects that span more than one week, use a calendar/planner showing 8-12 weeks, or more if needed. Block one- to three-hour chunks of your time for tasks and projects from start to finish.

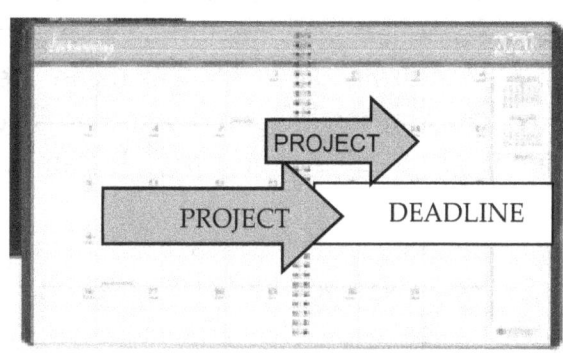

I like planners that show entire months, subdivided into weeks. You may prefer a big wall calendar. Just make sure you can flip ahead to future months to block out work time for big projects and see what's coming. You may prefer this to the IPO chart if most of your projects are long enough to spill over into future weeks and months.

If, however, your boss or customer has given you a deadline, flip ahead in your calendar to the deadline date and work your blocks of time backward to the current date. If you have worked back to the current date, and you're only on step seven, it's obvious you need to devote longer blocks or more blocks of time to the project.

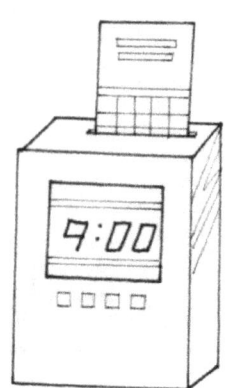

If this intrudes on the completion of other projects you have, then you need to review all of the projects you're working on and ask your boss or customer which project she or he agrees to delay.

This is preferable to suffering in silence and then making excuses when you can't meet the deadline. This makes your boss or customer part of the solution instead of part of the problem.

Now that you've assigned blocks of time to each step in the project, you are your own project manager. When someone asks, "Can we have a conference call Wednesday at 10:00 AM?" you can check your calendar for that day and reply, "No, I'm working on the Axon project then." Blocking your time on your calendar protects your time from less important requests for your time.

1. Set time targets for each task and each project.
2. When someone asks, "Do you have a minute?" your answer is, "No. I'm on a deadline," because you are. It's your own deadline and it carries the same importance as any other deadline.

Scheduling Tips to Avoid Burnout

HR professional Brenda Smith advises: "Just because you're working from home does not mean you should be working 24/7. You will burn out quickly. At the end of the day, log off completely from your computer and log back in the next morning. Anything in between can wait."

Brenda suggests breaks: "Take a lunch break, even if you're just folding laundry, paying bills or watching an afternoon program. Take a walk, make a call; it's your personal time. You do not have to be working or available 24/7."

Regarding personal time off, Brenda says, "Take your days off even if you are not going anywhere. This is so key to keeping your sanity! Doing nothing is not a sin."

Post Your Daily Work Hours

Finally, as we saw in chapter 3, create and post your own daily work hours. This lets the other people in your household know when to leave you alone.

~ Dad, we need bread.

~ I need a ride home from soccer practice.

To avoid interruptions, Aja Frost, author of *Work From Home Hacks*, advises a white board where your children, spouse, roommates etc. can write requests.

 **TIP**

Post your work hours.
Signs work wonders.

8. "Mommy, Where Do Deadlines Come From?"

Allison asks, "Mommy, where do deadlines come from?" "Here's how it happens," says Mommy, "The mommy asks the daddy, 'When will you finish repairing the wobbly dining room table?' and the daddy says, 'Soon.' 'Soon' means after watching two football games plus one weekend of flyfishing, plus other random man stuff. Then the mommy says, 'Your boss and her husband are coming to our house for supper this Friday.' Then the daddy says, 'Where are my %$&*#@ tools?' And that, Allison, is where deadlines come from."

Definition: deadline, *noun* (Merriam-Webster)

1. a line drawn around a prison that a prisoner passes at the risk of being shot [Oh my goodness!]

2. a time by which something must be done

Janis writes: That first definition is pretty scary. This word has come a long way, morphing into less-fatal uses, and we commonly accept the second definition. We use it all the time. It's one of our favorite ways to say no. "No, can't. I'm on a deadline." Case closed.

Deadlines Are Our Friends

Why?

1. A deadline is both the start and the end of planning our project work. It gets attention and respect from people who are working with you and from your own self.

    a. Sometimes we're given a deadline by a customer or boss. We place that on our calendars and plan backward, blocking enough time to get it done on time.

    b. If the project doesn't come with its own deadline, SET YOUR OWN. You have the power. You can plan out (see chapter 7) time for yourself and others to have something completed. A human being somewhere has set every deadline ever set. You're a human being. Do it.

2. Deadlines provide clear goals and expectations because they come with firm dates. There's nothing vague or fuzzy about a date on a calendar.

3. Deadlines provide excellent feedback along the way, as the calendar pages turn. We can SEE how we're progressing with just a glance.

4. Deadlines give us the opportunity to feel good and brag to everyone in sight (in other words, positive reinforcement for ourselves).

5. Setting your deadline, give yourself a comfy cushion of contingency time or "just in case" time. The rule of thumb from project managers is, add 20% contingency time.

6. Deadlines give us an irrefutable reason to say "No" to requests (we reiterate).

"I Work Best on a Deadline."

People who procrastinate often say, "I work best on a deadline." In that context, it often means they haven't started on the big report that's due tomorrow at 8:00 AM. "I work best on a deadline" can be like saying "I don't put gas in my car until the fuel gauge reads empty." This is dangerous because it assumes nothing else will interfere. Oops! My laptop got a virus the day before the deadline and I couldn't write the report, so I missed the deadline. There was a detour and my car burned extra gas on the way to the gas station and stopped in the middle of the intersection.

We ALL work best on deadlines. The difference is in work habits. Some people block enough time to meet or even beat the deadline. Then they work calmly and deliberately toward that magic date. Others burn the midnight oil to avoid missing the deadline. Same thing, you say? And what difference does it make?

Janis writes: In September, I set a deadline to design a video training program. I was to record the video on January 11. That meant creating hundreds of power point slides, writing my script, and rehearsing. I told myself I would start working on it after the holidays. "After the holidays" is a frequently spoken phrase by many businesspeople from Halloween on. It seems so far away. But when the day after Christmas arrived, "next year" somehow turned into just 16 days. Quel horreur!

Experts in training design say that it takes 40 hours of preparation for every (one) hour of training delivered. Thus, five hours of training takes 200 hours. So, I now have 16 days to do 200 hours of work, or 12.5 hours per day if I work all 16 days on this and don't do anything else.

I've now entered The Little Shop of Deadline Horrors. I've been telling myself (since September) that I have plenty of time "after the holidays." I'm in trouble. Oh, I'll get it done, of course. But will I have a life? How well will I sleep? And what will be the quality of the finished program?

But Meeting a Deadline is Meeting a Deadline, Right?

Meeting the deadline is meeting the deadline, right? The situation I had put myself into became a deadly deadline for me. I felt much more negative than positive for every one of those 16 days. Two+ weeks of my life made to be unhappy. Why did I let it happen?

Because the evil Dr. Procrastinasty is always lurking in the background, hoping to afflict us with

- Stress
- Worry
- Sleeplessness
- Energy and time spent thinking about it in the intervening weeks

Dr. Procrastinasty
Motto: Turning deadlines deadly

Procrastinating Can Produce Waste

- Work done in a hurry = mistakes
- Correcting mistakes = more time
- (the dreaded R word: rework)
- Delivering work full of mistakes = bad reputation for your work

Plan Time for the 3 Ps

Without planning ahead, I have no time for <u>proofreading</u>, <u>practicing</u>, or <u>polishing</u>. Hence, I'm not producing my best work for my customers, internal or external. Think of your due date not as a deadline, but a FINISH LINE.

Give yourself a comfy cushion of 20% contingency time. You'll probably BEAT your deadline!

🏈 The Goal Post 🏃

Sun.	Mon.	Tues.	Wed.	Thurs.	Fri.	Sat.
Week 1	Today				**Sub-goal 1:** Crunch sales data for all products	
Week 2				**Sub-goal 2:** Write analysis of each section of data		
Week 3		**Sub-goal 3:** Draft report for feedback by Chris & Erica			**Sub-goal 4:** Include feedback from Chris & Erica	
Week 4	**Sub-goal 5:** Proofread and polish	Contingency time "just in case"		**Project Deadline** **Submit!** ✔		

Raise your hand if you ever BEAT a deadline. I see hands going up! What a feeling, huh?

Deadlines are our friends. Deadlines are opportunities to celebrate, recognize the people who helped us succeed, and feel successful.

Deadlines   are   finish   lines!

Cheer!

Activate your *Finish-Line Vision* SuperPower. Keep your eye on the target date. Let it keep you focused on doing the work that will bring you to the finish line. Like a runner, one step at a time. One sub-goal at a time.

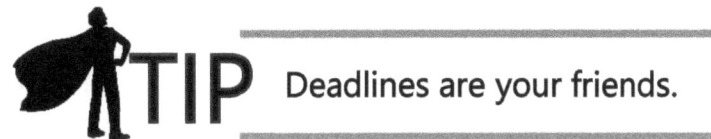

TIP   Deadlines are your friends.

9. Listen to Your Body Clock

Janis writes: In his book *When: The Scientific Secrets of Perfect Timing*, author Daniel Pink lends insights about the timing of your daily actions as well as the big events in your life (career moves, marital status, or where you live). Those are the big "whens." Let's focus on the close-up, daily "micro-whens" of our work from home—the daily decisions about what time we choose certain tasks. Here are some types of tasks and their best "when" matchups.

The Heavies. Big projects, close deadlines, or tasks you might be tempted to procrastinate:

1. **What time of the day** is it easiest for you to get "in flow" in your concentration and creativity? Use these times for your deep-thinking. For me, I need about 30 minutes of "feed-me time" after I get up in the morning. I feed both my body and my brain to become eager to dive into my work. Not just eating breakfast, but also reading something short and light—input to fuel my output. After

20 or so minutes of local news and weather, I've consumed all I need to put that light stuff away and start producing something.

I wait until I've worked for about two hours before checking my email. If I check it first thing, I'm off and running on some task that was not on my to-do list that day, and soon the day is half over. Dr.  Distracto is hiding in your email waiting to ambush you!

Don't check email yet!

What gets you going? Take a moment to think about it—if you had written the paragraph above, what would it say? What do you need to do, and how much time does it take?

2. **When** do you have both the fewest interruptions and the best mental alertness (the POWER)?

    a. 6:00 to 9:00 AM?
    b. Noon hour?
    c. 5:00 to 6:30 PM?
    d. 9:00 to 10:30 PM?

Grab this time for working on the heavies. Why? Interruptions give us an excuse to drop what we're doing and focus on that call, question, or notification. Turning our attention to those lighter temptations is more fun than staying immersed in

heavier lifting by our brains. There's more inherent reinforcement in doing things that are incompatible with the heavy work, so we want to set ourselves up to avoid those bright, shiny temptations.

The Lighter-Weights and Socials

When is your best time for meetings, phone calls, or in-person meetings? Fill these in around your heavies. Use these lighter-concentration tasks to give your brain a break, come up for air after working steadily for a few/several hours, and add some chunks of variety to your day.

 Also, tasks that involve other people tend to generate additional to-do items. After those, you might be galloping off on an unplanned path that can eat up most of your day. If you can schedule your heavies earlier in the day, you won't get to the end of your workday saying, "I didn't get anything on my list completed today. Argghhhh!"

Schedule your "heavies" earlier in the day.

What About Split Shifts?

During college, I worked as a cashier/hostess in a Red Lobster restaurant. I watched servers barrel in at 11:00 AM to prep for lunch, serve a full-house crowd, do their cleaning tasks, and leave around 2:30. Then many of them would show up again at 5:00 PM to do it all again for the dinner customers, finally leaving around 9:30. That schedule seems like a nightmare to some (me), but many of these folks told me they chose it and liked it.

This schedule enabled some to pick up their kids from school and spend time with them in the quiet of the afternoon. They used their early-morning time to do personal and household tasks, or errands on the way to the restaurant. Many of them worked this schedule four days a week, which earned them more (tips from 2 meals each day X 4=8) than if they'd worked only one meal for five or six days a week. Thus, they had the other three days off to enjoy their families and leisure time all day, plus more income!

Is a split shift for you? Some working-from-home folks find that similar split-shift schedules suit them and their family's needs, perhaps working after their kids are in bed. This, of course, depends on your energy level and ability to focus in the evening.

Don't Come Knockin' at My Door

Author Daniel Pink calls this "the hidden pattern of everyday life." To make these "when" decisions stick and to be most effective, let's bring them out of hiding. We can tell our family members, colleagues, customers, and friends about our personal schedules. We can ask them to contact us only during times we're open to interruptions and being with people: "I try to reserve mornings for deep-concentration work and prefer meetings and phone calls after 1:00, if that's convenient for you." Of course, you'll be open to making exceptions when necessary.

Quittin' Time

Make your "quittin' time" announcement at the end of your workday to help you transition from your work mentality to your laid-back self. Say it out loud to your family members as you and they breathe a happy sigh of relaxation.

As I power down my computer, I call out, "The office of Performance Leadership Consulting is now closed!" (even if I'm alone) as I prepare to go for a walk or eat and drink something (don't ask). As previously mentioned, one work-from-homer calls out, "Hi, honey, I'm home!" as she emerges from behind her folding screen.

You'll come up with your own fun way to celebrate the happy transition of a day's work well done and then enter your reward time.

Perform a test. Pick a one- or two-hour block of time for your heavies; mark it on your calendar for tomorrow and stick to it like glue. How did that work for you?

TIP Block two hours for your "heavies."
Test how it works for you.

10. Found Time

Janis writes: We all have times that require us to wait:

1. Uploading a document or video
2. You've logged in to your 10:15 AM TeamViewer meeting 10 minutes early to test your audio and make sure everything's working. (Excellent habit!) Now you have seven minutes while waiting for the host to start the meeting.
3. You're waiting at a restaurant for a colleague for a working lunch. (You might temporarily forget your annoyance at the person for being late if you concentrate on a task that makes you feel productive.)
4. You're in your car waiting to pick up your child from school.

What can you do while you're waiting?

Be Ready with *Fill-In* Tasks

It's useful to have in mind some short fill-in jobs that you can do while waiting.

1. If you're at home, these can be
   a. Hugging your child
   b. Bragging about something he's working on
   c. Short writing tasks
   d. Responding to emails
   e. 5S-ing your work area
   f. Stretching, walking, or lifting hand weights

2. If you're in your car, a bus, or a train, you might
   a. Dictate notes for a project you're working on
   b. Make your to-do list for tomorrow in a Notes app or an email to yourself
   c. Read a report that you've downloaded to your phone
   d. Make a call or send a text to schedule an appointment
   e. Phone Aunt Laurel just to say "Hi"

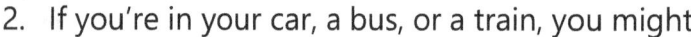

You might even jot down a list of these fill-in tasks. You can glance at your list when you find yourself waiting. Post the list in your work area and take a picture of the list to keep on your phone.

You might even enjoy putting a checkmark next to each activity when you do it. It's reinforcement for your personal productivity when you look at those checkmarks later.

Sequencing Your Tasks

Mike writes: I learned to do this while cooking breakfast. If I began cooking the eggs and bacon first and later started the coffee brewing, I ended up waiting for the  coffee to finish and the eggs got cold. I learned that coffee brewing takes the longest time. So, I start the coffee first and then move on to cooking bacon and eggs. This way, the coffee is ready to pour when the eggs are done and ready to serve hot. Sequencing eggs after starting the coffee makes everything hot and ready to serve at the same time.

My daughter, Shawn (pictured at right), used her waiting time (waiting for me to drive her to soccer practice) to play the piano. Smart girl! Playing the piano, she stayed patient, calm, and cheerful while she waited. So did Janis and I. Hearing her music, we were gently reminded with each note that we needed to get into the car soon and be on our way to soccer practice.

When you know you'll have waiting time, use it for non-urgent tasks. For example, use your waiting time in a doctor's office to catch up on emails and reading material.

 **TIP**

Use waiting time to
read your emails.

PART TWO:
COMMUNICATIONS

I WANT TO LIVE IN A WORLD WHERE EMAILS BURN CALORIES.

11. Email: Needles, Not Haystacks

Janis writes: *Don't Reply All* is the title of a book by Hassan Osman. His title says it all. The average knowledge worker spends 28% of his or her time on email, according to a study by McKinsey Global. That's more than 2½ hours a day—more than a quarter of the eight-hour workday! How much can we reduce this time and still get our business done effectively? Lots! Here's how to help our email recipients as well as ourselves:

1. **Don't Reply All.** Have you ever opened your mail to find 12 people's replies to a message, all stacked on top of each other like the mattresses in the Hans Christian Andersen children's story "The Princess and the Pea?" In the story, a queen wanted to determine if a certain girl was a real princess. She stacked a dozen mattresses on top of a tiny pea for the girl to sleep on, to see if the girl was as sensitive to a "lump"' in the bed as a true princess would be. (I won't tell you the exciting ending.)

Wading through other people's "reply all" responses is like trying to get to the pea under multiple layers and is a huge waste of your time (and your 11 co-workers' time). So please don't tap that "reply all" button unless you're absolutely certain all those people are just dying to read what you've written.

1. **Use the Heck Out of Your Subject Line.** State as much of your message as possible. This lets the receiver know what to begin thinking about. If a task has a deadline, include the target date and time. Example: *Please send specs for product #8542 by July 18. EOM* (EOM means end of message and signals: "No need to open this email.")

> **EOM is a welcome acronym for busy people.**

2. **Set a Deadline for the Reply or Completion of Action Items.** Put this in your subject line to alert your recipient before he even opens your message. Deadlines help both the sender and receiver to plan. Banish "ASAP" from your vocabulary and from the Earth. "As Soon As Possible" means different things to different people. When the requester writes ASAP, she means, "Drop everything and do this." When the receiver sees ASAP, he assumes, "Whenever I can work this into everything else I have to do." ASAP is sure to disappoint and annoy both parties.

> **Banish ASAP.**

3. **Number Your Points and Requests Rather Than Burying Them in Paragraphs.** Thirty-year business owner Kathy Peterson says, "In all my years of emailing, I've come to the conclusion that people only seem to answer the beginning of an email, especially if it is long. If there is more than one question you need answered, number the list so it is obvious that you need your recipient to address all of it. That way, you can respond with, "How about #4-6?"

Numbering your questions or requests saves your recipients a truckload of time. No wasted time re-reading to pick out the action items needed or the important information. A numbered list becomes an efficient and easy-to-read **checklist**, giving visual feedback to the responder that she's completed two of the three items, for instance, and has one remaining.

Checklists are great tools because they provide

a. clear expectations;
b. feedback on our progress in completing the items;
c. positive reinforcement for getting the items done.

(These are all the keys to great performance!)

Paragraphs are haystacks. Numbered lists are needles.

The *things to do* are the needles. Don't set up a time-wasting, needle-in-a-haystack search for busy people on the receiving end of your email.

Ever received an email like the one below?

> **To: All**
> **From: Mr. Haystack**
> **Subject: Something to think about**
> Over the last few months, it has come to the attention of many of our stakeholders that we could become a much more efficient operation if we took full advantage of our burgeoning unlimited resources to crowdsource from varying entities. Let us collaborate to look globally for inspiration. Every team member is requested to engage and participate in this unprecedented initiative. I value your considered opinions and look forward to your enlightened engagement.

AARGH!!!!! I still don't know what he wants me to DO!
Now look at the email below.

> To: Gail and Mike
> From: Janis
> Subject: Request improvements to preface by 2/2
> Gail and Mike,
> 1. Would you please make improvements to this draft for me?
> 2. I'd like your changes by Feb. 2 at 5 pm.
> My thanks, Janis

Short, to the point, and tells you **WHAT** to **DO** by **WHEN**.

Aren't you glad this chapter contains numbered items, not just haystack paragraphs?

4. **Be Bold and Colorful.** Graphic artist Kathy Peterson advises, "If there is an attachment, point it out by telling your receiver the file name or bold/underline: "See attached PDF," etc. A change of text color is also a great way to point out the important things/questions."

5. **Reply Inline**. Click reply and type your answers right into the original email, under each of the sender's points or requests. Make your replies a different color or use ALL CAPS to make them stand out and easy to read. This saves you the time of composing an opening, "In response to your questions about . . ." and enables the originator to see that all his questions have been answered. Like the checklist created by numbering, it is quick, visual feedback to feel confident that everything's taken care of, or that there's one outstanding item to follow up on.

6. **Be Brief.** Challenge yourself for one day to limit your emails to six sentences. Doesn't that feel great? Do it again the next day. House designer Stephen Jackson said, "My emails may come off as curt to some clients, but I assume people are busy and appreciate brevity." Amen! **Be brief, be brilliant, be gone.**

7. **Email Instead of Calling.** Emails almost always takes less time than a phone conversation and provide a written document for both sender and receiver, to refer to later. It also gives you time to think, edit, and revise your reply if you wish.

8. **Limit and "Group" Your Email Time.** "Only check your email at certain times of day—don't let it interrupt your work," advises Professor Shawn McCarthy. Perhaps first thing in the morning and mid-afternoon, or times that work for you. To make this work, you'll need to remove the temptation of those noxious noises from that Nefarious Dr. Notification! When you turn on notifications, you have created

> Turn off notifications—
> those noxious noises from
> the nefarious
> Dr. Notification.

your own two-year-old toddler constantly tugging on your sleeve with, "Mommy, Mommy" or "Daddy, Daddy." But unlike the two-year-old, you can turn notifications off.

9. **Don't Let Your Inbox Dictate Your Priorities.** Here's some cautionary advice from the book, *Secrets of the Remote Workforce: By Employees. For Employees.* by Teresa Douglas, Holly Gordon, and Mike Webber:

> "Avoid checking email as the first task of your day. Email is like oxygen for most people who work remotely: We need it to function and survive. The problem is that many people in the virtual workforce get a high volume of email. If you check your

email first thing, you run the risk of completing tasks *in the order in which they appear in your inbox*, rather than in order of importance. Over time, that experience can be incredibly draining.

"Instead of making your inbox your first stop, it may be more beneficial to have a list of tasks that you need to accomplish. And let that list prioritize your time."

Gail writes: ALWAYS answer emails, if only with a brief reply. Not doing so is extremely discourteous in my view. I've sent multiple emails to people whose names I was given to interview. Some never answered after 20 emails. I remember W.C. Field's comment: "If at first you don't succeed, try, try again. Then quit. No point in making a damn fool of yourself." A short reply, even one of disinterest, would have been appreciated, so I could mark the person off my list. When I finally give up on an interviewee, I explain it this way: "There's a fine line between persistence and stalking!"

Double-read all messages before you hit send. Auto correct can kill you. If angry, wait another day. Back in the earlier days of autocorrect,

Auto correct can kill you.

I wrote an email to a client who had been very gracious to me, taking me on a tour of her facility, and introducing me to interviewees. Her name was Becky, and in an attempt to be personal, I included her name throughout my message: "Thank you so much for your time Becky. It was so nice to meet you Becky." Just as I was about to hit send, I saw that every *Becky* had been replaced with *Bitchy*. To this day, I get heart palpitations when I think about how horrible it would have been if I had sent that email! This cautionary tale applies to text messages as well. As I recently said to a friend, "Autocorrect on text has probably done more damage than a simple typo could ever do!"

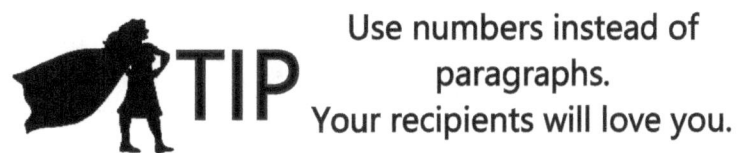

Use numbers instead of paragraphs.
Your recipients will love you.

12. Phone Calls: Chatty or Concise?

Janis writes: Tips for phone calls are the same as for emails: *Be Brief, Be Brilliant, Be Gone.*

Be Brief

My cousin, Dot Allen, ended our phone conversation with a sharp "Bye." The next thing I heard was a click. I had been in the middle of a sentence, so I called her back and said, "Hey, Dot. I wasn't finished." She said, "I was." I laughed and wrapped up my story in a hurry, hoping to get it all in before the next "Bye!"

I was laughing about this on a call with another cousin, who asked, "She said 'bye' to you? She just hangs up on me! So, consider yourself lucky." Ha ha. I told Dot about our cousin's little joke. She laughed. This became part of our family culture. All my cousins now try to be the first to say "Bye!"

When I wrote a memoir of family stories, I asked Dot's permission to use this story. She not only gave permission, but she marked "her" story's page in the book with a sticky note so she could show it to every visitor who came into her home. I think Dot was onto something about managing her time (and proud of it!).

We can always add a transition phrase like, "Talk to you later," before the abrupt "Bye!" but Dot will always be there as our role model.

Gail writes: If the phone call is for an interview or meeting, write out your questions ahead. After the talk and maybe a bit of chit-chat, you can always politely end the conversation by asking, "Is there anything I haven't asked you or that we haven't discussed that you'd like to add?" This usually segues/ends the interview in a positive way.

Of course, sometimes you have to break the rule of talking too long, like when a CEO started crying over the phone, telling me about his little dog dying. Ya gotta stay human after all.

Phone or Email?

Janis writes: I prefer email to calls because they're faster to write, faster to read, and force the writer (including me) to be more precise and less repetitive. But sometimes calls are necessary, so let's make the most of them efficiency-wise with some great points from Carnegie Mellon Professor Randy Pausch's lecture, "Time Management."
http://www.cs.virginia.edu/~robins/Randy/TMenglishTranscript.pdf

Pausch says:

1. "Start your phone calls by announcing your goals for the call.
   'Hi, Jason. Two things. One is . . .'
   'Later: 'The second thing is . . .'
   "This sets the expectation with Jason that you have a crisp agenda in mind and holds you accountable for sticking with it. Telling the number of topics you want to discuss keeps both of you on track."

2. "The telephone can be a great time waster . . . so I recommend standing during the phone calls. Great for exercise, and if you tell yourself, 'I'm not gonna sit down until the call is over,' you'll be amazed how much brisker you are."

3. "I find that calling somebody at 11:50 is a great way to have a ten-minute phone call. Because frankly, you may think you're interesting, but you are not more interesting than lunch."

Take charge of your time. Traditional etiquette has been that the person initiating the call is the one who ends the call. Forget that. Even if you're the "callee" rather than the caller, you can end the call. Don't drag it out or apologize with long explanations. Rip the band-aid off.

"Thanks for calling." (Short pause) "Bye."
"Well, back to my project. Talk to you later."
"Thanks for calling. Bye."

Ever hoped you'd get someone's voicemail?

Raise your hand if you've ever crossed your fingers in hopes that you'd get someone's voicemail rather than the person. That's evidence that we *know* phone calls take too much of our time.

Many work-at-homers say what they miss most is social contact. If you crave these chats, by all means, linger longer. You decide your priorities.

Make Your Calls Work Efficiently for You

Before you initiate a call, jot down what you want to achieve. Keep your notes in front of you during the call and glance down for self-feedback on how you're doing in the time you've spent so far.

If you're speaking to a chatty timewaster, jump in right away by stating the purpose of your call and a clear signal that it's business: "Hey, just a quick question. Who will be working on the business development team?" You may have to act fast with some people to beat them to the "talk."

When you answer a call from a chatty person, ask, "What can I do for you?" or "How can I help you?" It signals your generous willingness to help, but also says, "Let's get to business."

Voicemail Is Your BFF

"Why did you answer the phone?"
"Because it rang."

A friend often says (ironically) when he hears a phone ring during a lunch date or a meeting: "Better answer that. It might be the phone." Exactly. It's just a phone.

Many of us are programmed to answer all ringing phones automatically, no matter who the caller is (or even if unknown) or what we're in the middle of.

When you're concentrating on an important report, in a meeting, or solving a sticky problem, don't let that cool ringtone seduce you into answering if you need to be focusing on something or someone else. Once you interrupt  yourself, you lose not only the 15 minutes spent on the call, but four to five more minutes getting your head back into your work. You could forget that brilliant thought you were on the cusp of writing, or that new solution to a chronic problem.

Return calls when you need a walk-around break and some social contact later in your workday. Timing is everything.

Your phone is not your master. It's a tool, like a screwdriver, whose purpose is to make your job easier, not to rule your life. You use *it,* don't let it use you.

**The phone serves you.
You don't serve the phone.**

13. Death by Meeting?

Janis writes: *Death by Meeting* is the title of a book by Patrick Lencioni. There's a reason. Meetings can be murderers of our time. Maybe you've whispered, "I'm bored to death," "I'm dying to get out of this meeting!" or "This stupid discussion is killing me." So many death-wishes connected to meetings!

So many death wishes connected to meetings!

A July 2020 study of 3,143,270 (yes, three million) remotely working knowledge workers for the National Bureau of Economic Research revealed an average of 11.5% *less* time spent in meetings compared to 2019.

Perhaps that's because there are so few in-person meetings now and attendees are distracted with their other projects visible beside their screens. Perhaps it's due to the meeting platforms offering free meetings of up to 40 minutes but charging a fee after that. Or both leaders and attendees might be treating the meetings more formally to get work done rather than let the discussion wander or socialize? Something to ponder. What do you think?

Working remotely, you want to make the best use of all your time: personal and business, solo and in groups. When you have control of meeting decisions, be sure to use your time and your attendees' time to create value. Let's hold a magnifying glass over meeting traditions and see if we can make them more effective and efficient.

Standing Meetings

No, this doesn't mean that you're on your feet during the meeting. "Standing" in this case means a meeting that repeats every Monday or every morning, also called *recurring*. Carnegie Mellon Professor Randy Pausch described the following cartoonish scene outside a meeting room. "Someone asked, 'Why are we here?' Answer: 'Because we're having a meeting. *It's on all of our calendars.*'"

Pausch quipped, "It's just a classic Dilbert moment: 'We're having a meeting because it's on our calendars.' Or 'It's on our calendars because we're having a meeting.'" You get the point of this circular reasoning.

> **"Why are we meeting?"**
> **"Because it's on the calendar."**

Have you ever been suckered into putting "standing meetings" (every Friday or whatever) on your calendar? A "standing" meeting puts the meeting first, before you even know what it's for. Standing meetings sometimes take on a life of their own. Scary!

Make Sure Your Meetings PRODUCE Something

One time Mike asked a new client for a meeting. The client opened his planner and asked, "What's the agenda?" Mike answered, "I don't have one yet." "Get back to me when you do," the client said as he closed his planner. Now there was a person in control of his time—my hero! The act of closing his planner said it all.

We can ensure that our meetings are worth our time if we use "Russell's Rules of Outcomes." Performance consultant Russell Justice requires every meeting to have a written DESIRED OUTCOME. Not just a "purpose." Not just an agenda.

Russell's requirement for holding or attending a meeting is to complete this sentence: "At the end of this meeting, we will HAVE _____ (desired outcomes)."

"At the end of this meeting we will HAVE _____."

For example, "At the end of this meeting, we will HAVE a plan to roll out our new service, including action items, dates due, and names of team members who will do these action items."

The beauty of this tool is that, at the end of the meeting, you know if you've created your desired outcome, or what percentage of it you've accomplished.

You know the meeting was worth your (and four other people's) time or it wasn't. Meetings are like buckets. They're a container for carrying something of value. The thing of value is what's created in the meeting.

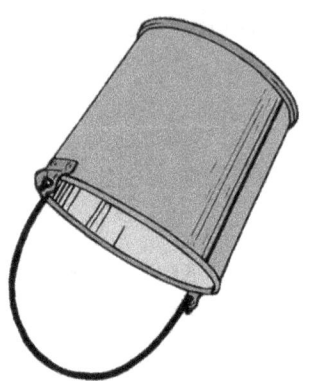

Without having a way to define and measure the thing of value, you'll walk out of the meeting with an empty bucket.

Defeat the Evil Dr. Zoom

We asked work-from-homers, "Videoconferencing: love or hate?"
What they said they don't like:

1. The delay in voice communication, so we step on other people talking
2. Can't see non-verbal cues or facial expressions well
3. When some attendees' equipment isn't working and others must wait

What people do like:

1. It's a way to get business done from home.
2. It provides some social interaction. (One working-from-homer who craves more social interaction even said she'd be willing to go back to those boring in-person meetings just to be with people and hear the "shop talk.")

> Zoom – everyone is looking at you all the time.

Mike writes: Zoom and other video conferencing apps take more energy, because you are "on stage" all the time. Everyone is looking at you all the time. If you look away for an instant, it looks like you are off task. If the Zoom camera can focus on that trashy beach novel on the bookshelf behind you, everyone thinks you've been goofing off. When you were at the office in the conference room, not everybody was watching everybody else all the time. Zoom becomes "Big Brother is Watching You" times ten.

- Think you can get away with wearing pajamas? No! You are on camera.
- Think you can talk to your dog? No! You are on audio.

We have all seen these little Zoom reality TV shows of children, spouses, dogs and cats entering camera range and uttering their lines for a cameo role in the show. Each screen credit adds to their acting resume!

To defeat the evil Dr. Zoom, you must be prepared to do the following:
- Keep your video camera turned off if you don't want to be seen.
- Learn how to activate the background to block views of your room.
- Keep your audio microphone turned off until you want to speak.
- Post a sign "Quiet please! Videoconference in progress."
- Keep your door closed to keep out cats, toddlers, and husbands.

Screen Fatigue Is a Real Thing

Libby Sander and Oliver Bauman wrote about video fatigue (May 26, 2020 on Essential Millenial.com). https://www.essentialmillennial.com/zoom-fatigue/

"People feel like they have to make more emotional effort to appear interested, and in the absence of many non-verbal cues, the intense focus on words and sustained eye contact is exhausting."

Also, as noted above, on a videoconference, we can never glance away without fear of another person thinking we're distracted or not interested in the meeting. When we're in-person, it's considered natural body language to glance away occasionally. On video, we have to be "on" all the time.

Be careful. Prepare for the Call.

Advice from Karen Adamedes, author of *Professional in Pajamas*. "Be sure your notifications are turned off when you'll be sharing your screen. No one wants to see a pop-up every time you receive an email." Also, if your email shows the first couple of lines of the message, you may be in for a red face!

Adamedes also warns to close all the tabs you had open before the online meeting. "It's too easy to flick between screens and show something you don't want to share."

Dress for Success

Your choice of clothing signals your level of respect for other attendees.

No, this isn't a throwback to the days of suits and stockings. But resist the temptation to show up on the meeting screen in an old t-shirt or pajama top. Your choice of clothing signals your level of respect for the other meeting attendees. Wear the same thing you would wear if you were in person. If you're not dressed appropriately, turn off your camera for the Zoom call.

Set Your Limits

I was invited to a two-hour online meeting from 2:00 to 4:00 AM with prospective clients for a wide-ranging planning discussion. After the first hour, I realized much of the discussion didn't concern me, and I was zoning out and contributing little. The next week, I was invited again to this client's "standing" meeting. I responded that I would be available from 2:00 to 3:00. The agenda items involving me were covered during that time and I bowed out. No one asked questions or expected me to stay longer. Everybody won.

> Ask "Is there another way?" before booking meetings.

Convert Meetings to Email

First, convert proposed meetings to email communications whenever possible. And think BIG and assertively about this possibility. For every videoconference topic you can handle via email, you have saved perhaps as much as 50% of the time required by you if you were on this meeting. Can you and your colleagues achieve your desired outcome with some method other than a meeting?

- Email?
- Document-sharing?
- Phone call with fewer people?

No-Meeting Days

1. Pick one or two days each week that you designate as "no-meeting" days. Mark them on your calendar. Protect them for projects where you need to concentrate. It feels good to wake up in the morning and realize you have no meetings—that the whole day is yours.

2. Group your meetings on the other days of the week.

Oh, the joy of a blank day on your calendar!

Be a Leader

If you're in a meeting with lots of discussion that doesn't seem to be leading anywhere, ask, "Do we have a decision we can write down?" or "Is there an action item to be noted here?" Even if you're a lowly attendee, not the leader, others will appreciate your initiative to move the process along and get everyone's money's worth out of their valuable time. Don't let bad meetings happen to good people.

TIP Don't let bad meetings happen to good people.

PART THREE:

YOUR WORK HABITS

14. Procrastinate Your Procrastinating

Mike writes: Ever put together a jig-saw puzzle? If you were to look only at the hundreds of random pieces, you would be tempted to . . . procrastinate! The evil Dr. Procrastinasty (pictured at right) just shot you with his *put-it-off* venom.

Dr. Procrastinasty

But . . .

if you look at the picture on the box cover at left, you see the big picture (end result) you are working toward. You see golden sky on the upper righthand side of the picture, and you begin to look for gold pieces to place on that side. You see blue mountains on the middle right, and you begin to look for blue pieces.

The big picture is PULLING you, piece by piece, into the task. You look for outlines and colors. You say to yourself, "I'm going to fill in all the blue mountain pieces and then continue tomorrow." You do the big job *one section at a time.*

Stephen Covey, Author of *The 7 Habits of Highly Successful People,* suggested "begin with the end in mind." The big picture = the end result. Make a big picture for yourself. Make a list of what the completed project will look like. That's your big picture. Find a task or topic that pulls your interest. Begin right there.

Getting started with this book, Janis laid out cards with our chapter topics on a big rug (photo at right). She made a big "jigsaw puzzle" of what the finished book would look like. This big picture began pulling me into

chapter topics. I looked it over and thought, "I have some ideas for that one." I began writing and soon I had a chapter done.

When finished, we printed the pages and placed them on the card for that chapter topic—one more puzzle piece filled in! We can **see** it filling in. "We're making progress," we said to each other.

Starting by doing one small task means you have dodged the deadly put-it-off pellet from Dr. Procrastinasty's postponement pistol. Every sub-task you complete protects you from his dithering, vacillating, dilly-dallying, shilly-shallying procrastination pellet.

Dr. Procrastinasty's Other Poison Pellet: Internet Search-Surfing

Janis writes: I'm a writer. I like writing once I get into an idea or a project. But if I run across an idea or product or book or app that I want to find out more about, I'm tempted to pause my writing to do a search. Doing searches is fun and doesn't require as much concentration because I'm consuming information instead of producing information. More fun!

To prevent myself from going off on this extraneous excursion prematurely, I make a deal with myself: When I finish this chapter, page, or module, I'll save my work and search for that shiny new thing. It always works to get me working faster so I can get to my reward.

Antidote: The Premack Pill

Dr. David Premack (a behavior researcher) noticed that if you reward yourself <u>after</u> doing stuff you DON"T like to do by giving yourself permission to do stuff you DO like to do, then the stuff you normally avoid and procrastinate gets done more often.

Do tasks you don't like FIRST, then do tasks you <u>do like</u> SECOND = you get more done. I like getting out of the house, usually by running errands in town. I do my authoring tasks in the morning and reward myself with a trip to town in the afternoon. Taking Dr. Premack's "pill," this is how I get more work done.

PREMACK PILL

Gail writes: My DNA stands for, "Do Not Avoid!" I've always hated to have assignments hanging over my head at school or at work, because the thought of it tortured me—a bit OCD (Obsessed with Completing Deadlines). My schoolmates hated me for it, but in college, while they were stressing over a last-minute paper, I was having a beer at the bar.

My DNA stands for "Do Not Avoid!"

Not a beer drinker? Other rewards: Take a hot shower! Put a few pieces in a jig-saw puzzle (the closest I'll ever get to meditation). Read, read, read: my favorite. Call a friend. Step outside and get some sun!

Janis writes: Below are tasks I'm tempted to procrastinate (and ways I nudge myself into getting them done):

1. **Tasks I don't have much experience with.** I feel self-conscious when I haven't picked up the skills to glide through a new software while all my colleagues are humming away on it, so I tend to bury my head in the sand. But once I felt brave enough to ask a colleague to coach me. She happily (I think) agreed, answered  my dumb questions, taught me how to correct my errors, and suggested a tutorial. Pretty soon I was able to take this off my "ugly" list and stop procrastinating. **Solution: Ask for help.**

2. **Humungous projects**. When the monster project is staring you in the face, "make ready." The concept of making ready comes from manufacturing, where job standards include time for employees to prepare for a job: get the materials needed, lay out the tools, and study the instructions. It's prepping, just like making an outline or a list of requirements before starting a project. Once you've "made ready," the next step seems easier. And before you know it, you're working on step five and have forgotten how impossibly big this project seemed. **Solution: Make ready.**

3. "On the fence" decisions. Putting off decisions causes me to feel stress. Thinking and worrying about them again and again is time wasted. Should I send this document now or edit it more first? Take these shoes to the consignment store or keep them another season? Follow up with that prospective new client or wait a few days? Take that new job or stay put?

Big life-changing decisions (job change, relationship change, buy a house, etc.) deserve much research, budgeting, and the seeking of advice.

 Smaller decisions often consume an inordinate amount of our time compared to the impact they'll have. If a decision can be amended later, that's a factor in favor of making a decision without allowing it to consume you. Some questions I ask myself when I'm stuck on smaller decisions:

- How important is it that this be a *perfect* decision?
- Can it be changed if needed?
- Will life be OK either way?
- Will anybody remember this five years from now?
- Can I do a small test? (Reversible)

I always feel relief to unload that small, "this is not rocket surgery" decision and get on with focusing 100% of my time on my priorities. **Solution: Just do it.**

4. **Calling someone with bad news or a delicate subject** never gets better by waiting. In fact, it's like fish, smelling worse every day. So, I do two things:

   a. Get the person's phone number in front of me on paper, or have my contacts opened to his or her name.

   b. Jot down bullet points I want to communicate, ending with a question to get his or her ideas.

These two simple actions (aka "making ready") ease me into this unpleasant, dreaded task, especially the notes I've written down. Having sort of a script helps me get into the bad news or delicate topic smoothly—I just read what's in front of me as directed (by me). As soon as the other person responds, I'm at ease and we're working together on solutions. AND I get to cross this ugly task off my list. Hooray! **Solution: Write your script.**

4. **Take that (ugh) medicine.** I found that if I gulp it down early in the day, I can stop dreading it and, as they say in the grocery store, "Have a nice day." "Do the ugliest thing first," advises Professor Randy Pausch. These tasks are "ugly" because we don't want to do them. We'd like to walk around with blinders on and pretend they don't

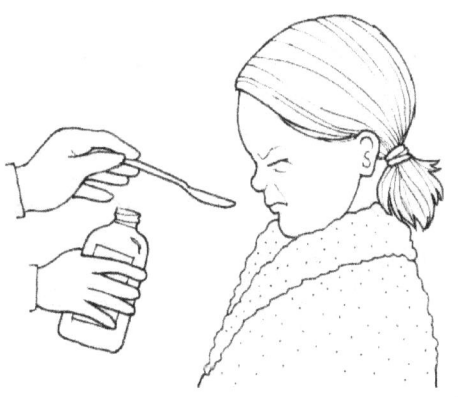

exist. But ignoring those ugly little boogers won't make them go away. **Solution: Do the ugliest thing first.**

There is usually an inverse relationship between how much something is on your mind and how much it's getting done. —David Allen, author, *Getting Things Done*

Mike writes: Next up - Dr. Procrastinasty's brother, the evil Dr. Distracto, the devious, demanding deliverer of distractions that prevent us from focusing on our priority projects. Dr. Distracto dumps deliciously tempting activities that encourage us to doom our deadlines. When you allow distractions, you are procrastinating!

Dr. Distracto

Examples of distractions:

- **Junk email.** *"Oh, my gosh. I've won an Amazon gift card for $100! How many clicks does it take to claim it? 56? I'll do it."*
- **Junk mail.** *"An invitation to a fancy dinner—free—all I have to do is listen to a 30-minute presentation about vacation homes. Just fill out this form. Three pages? I'm on it."*

When you allow distractions, you are procrastinating!

- **Housemates**. *"Have you seen my plaid pajamas? I have a Zoom call and I have to look good."* Me: *"I think I saw them somewhere. I'll help you look."*
- **Object in peripheral vision**. *"There's the candle Aunt Pettybone gave us for Christmas and I never wrote her a thank-you note. I'll do that now."*
- **Children**: *"Tell Will to stop knocking over my Legos!"* Me: *"Here, I'll help you build your tower back."*
- **Text message**. *"Got a minute? I need your opinion on which font to use for this proposal."*
- **Voicemail from Uncle Barnacle**. *"Bless his heart. I'll call him and chat for just a minute."*
- **A dust bunny on the floor**. *"I'll just pick that up. Maybe I should vacuum the whole house?"*

The list is endless, but you must resist. How?

1. Remove everything from your workspace except the items you need to do your work.
2. Remove all icons from your computer screen except those for your files and programs you use to do your work.
3. Set your internet search screen to blank. No news-site defaulting allowed.
4. Enforce workspace boundaries and the times you're not available.
5. Keep your work document on the screen in front of you.

CAUTION: If you contract a severe case of *distractivitis*, from Dr. Distracto, you may need this ANTI-DISTRACTION VISOR. It will block the glare, (preventing eyestrain), block views of potato chip bags (preventing willpower strain) and all other dastardly distractions. Just call 1-800-DISTRACTO. Operators are standing by to take your order.

"Make Ready" helps you fight off the evil Dr. Procrastinasty and Dr. Distracto. Soon you'll give yourself the "completed" stamp of approval.

Gail writes: I encountered a real Dr. Distracto one day on my way to the bank. This was one of those necessary errands that I completed during my "lunch break." As I drove down our rural road, I noticed a car pulled off on a side road. I saw a man in the driver's seat with his head back, mouth open, and eyes closed. I kept driving but my imagination started talking: "What if he had a heart attack?" "Nah," I answered. "He's probably just taking a break." On my trip back, I slowed down, and he was still in the same position. I pulled over to our little, local mart and told the man behind the counter that maybe we should call someone. He proceeded to do so, and I left, thinking I'd done my part.

Four days later, my husband Jack and I went into the same store and the clerk said to me, "You remember that guy you told me about? I called the people who own the hardware store near there and who operate that landfill. They went to check on him and turned out he was an undercover agent who was trying to catch them for illegal dumping. He was plenty mad because you blew the whole thing."

He was an undercover agent!

"Well, then he shouldn't have been sleeping on the job!" I said. As we left the store, Jack asked me, "What the heck do you *do* during the day?!"

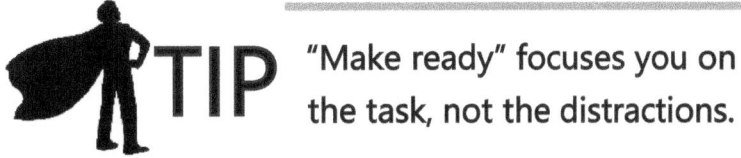

TIP "Make ready" focuses you on the task, not the distractions.

15. Weed Out Your Time Wasters

Janis writes: On a typical workday, you may do a lot of stuff that doesn't help you reach your goals. In other words, time wasters. Some time wasters are spontaneous interruptions; some are events or actions you've gotten into the habit of doing and continue to do even though they're no longer useful or enjoyable to you. Habits are hard to break!

Do you have standing commitments that you wish you didn't "have" to perform or attend? Events or groups you've gotten into the habit of helping, but that feel more like an obligation you don't want to spend time on now (five years later, perhaps)?

Don't allow the finite resource of your precious time to go into the wastebasket. Wasted time is something you can never get back.

Consider:

1. Just stop doing the activities.

2. Find a way to accomplish the mission in a shorter time.

3. With the person involved, brainstorm other settings and methods, such as the following:

   - Walk while you meet; (get some exercise and Vitamin D!).
   - Have a phone conference instead of in-person meetings.
   - Make plans and conduct your follow-up via email.

4. Make a list of the activities that waste your time:

   - Notifications from your devices
   - People wanting to tell you "what they're going through"
   - Social media
   - Watching the news
   - Snacking

Each day, pick one of these to "weed out." If you're not ready to pull it out by its roots, prune it back to a smaller amount of time wasted, or a less-frequent occurrence: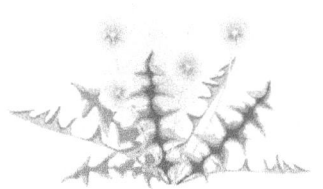

1. Shape your behavior gradually: Reduce your time spent on this time waster by 50%, then 75%, then 100%.

2. Cut the frequency of an event in half: make it every two weeks instead of every week, or every-other day instead of daily.

Here are some examples:

Time Wasters I Can Weed Out (Or at Least Prune Back)		
The Culprit	**Weed or Prune & How?** (pick a method from previous page)	**Date weeded out** or began pruning
Answering phone if it's an unknown caller or personal call during working hours	This is why God made voicemail and the OFF button on your phone. Use it!	
Interrupting myself when notifications sound	Turn off notifications.	
Wasting time on social media	Delete accounts or use social media time as a reward when you've completed your to-do list.	
Chatty Charlies	Let calls go to voicemail and answer via text or email. "I'm on deadline. Gotta go."	
Procrastinating	Perform ONE small step to "make ready" to tackle the project. For example, lay out the materials or just make a list of what you need to research.	
Your examples		

Don't Get Trapped

I once had a friend who would call and ask, "Are you doing anything Saturday?" Fumbling for several seconds, I would say no, mumble something about checking my calendar, or not being sure. Then she would reveal what she wanted me to do. Maybe see a movie, maybe help her move, maybe help with a fund-raiser, maybe spend time with a group of friends.

Often it would be something I didn't want to do, but I hadn't said no yet. Her question, "Are you doing anything Saturday?" was still hanging out there and wouldn't go away. So, I'd promise to check my calendar and get back to her. For several hours or days, I wondered how to say no, because I hadn't told her up front that I was busy.

Finally, I realized what was happening. She had been making an open-ended request for my time before telling me what my time would be used for. I was aghast. Not at her, but at myself for falling into that unknown time after time. After a little talk with myself and much rehearsing, I was prepared to reply to her with my own question, "What did you have in mind?" or "Why? What's happening?" Then, _after_ she revealed the reason she was asking, I could say, "I think I'll pass on that this time," or "That's not a project I want to tackle. Good luck with it," or just "No, thanks."

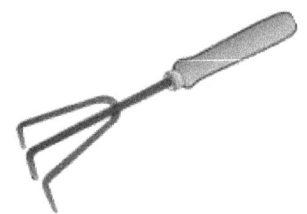

Being ready with my comeback helps me avoid the agony of dragging out the reply plus assertively reserving my time for ONLY things I really want to do.

Can't wait to miss it!

Gail writes: Understanding my avoidance of large crowds and fancy affairs, my good friends are used to my reply, "Can't wait to miss it!"

*Weed out your time-wasters
and don't look back.*

16. Let Go

Janis writes: "What would happen if I don't do this?" This is a great question suggested by Professor Randy Pausch. How many tasks do you keep doing

- just because you've always done them (out of habit)—without asking yourself or anyone else if these tasks are still needed;
- because no one else seems to be stepping up;
- because you didn't know a different way to get this mission accomplished—other than expending <u>your</u> time and energy?

There's an old story about a man who always cut off and discarded two inches from the end of a beef roast before putting it into the pan. Finally, someone asked why he was wasting that good meat. "That's how my mother always cooks her roasts," he answered. The next time he talked to his

mother he asked her why. "My roasting pan is too small. It's the only way the roast will fit in," she explained. The man realized he'd been doing a wasteful practice his whole adult life without knowing why. His roasting pan was big enough, but he imitated his mother without questioning the practice.

It can be valuable to question every habit we have and test its usefulness by putting these assumptions to the test:

1. **No one can do it as well as I would**. I have to check behind everything my co-worker, children, spouse, roommate, or partner does. They're probably not checking reports or packing lunches as well as I would.

   Perform a test. For one day, put down your magnifying glass and step away from your micro-manager persona. Did anyone go hungry? Was the report correct? Did the world come to an end? If not, you can continue to let go of all this checking and snooping.

2. **If I don't do it, it won't get done**. I took on the responsibility of scheduling volunteers for a non-profit organization. This was on top of two other ongoing responsibilities for that organization, but I assumed no one else would do it, so I jumped on it first and did the scheduling for a year. I became increasingly tired and demotivated because I had volunteered to do too much.

The next season, I kept my mouth shut and sat on my hands at the pre-season planning meeting. Guess what? Another person volunteered, circulated a sign-up sheet, and took care of this whole time-consuming but important job for the next two years and counting—a job well done!

Why did I think I was the only one who would volunteer? It's about time in my life to start giving other people more credit and respect!

TIP: Challenge yourself to keep your mouth closed at the next opportunity to volunteer. Is the work (eventually if not immediately) getting done?

Bonus: You can acquire a "follower" persona in exchange for your "leader" reputation. Wear it proudly (and quietly) and add it to your resume.

3. **Does the customer want this?** A designer of greeting cards selling online decided he would send a follow-up email to each customer, asking them to complete a 10-question survey about the product designs and delivery experience. He began to receive write-in comments from his customers, telling him that the long surveys were an annoyance. He stopped sending the surveys.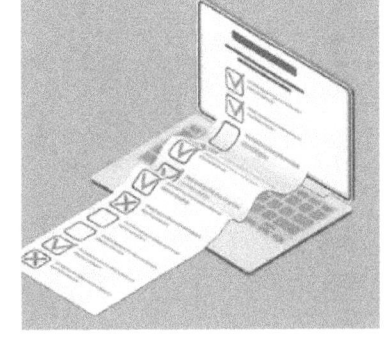

Wow. Think of the time he could've saved if he'd learned this valuable information six or nine months earlier. Scrutinize everything you and your company do to produce your product or service by asking, "Does this add value to the customer?" This goes for all those above-and-beyond practices you use at home as well. (Are you still ironing your towels?)

Letting go is an exhilarating feeling. It's like cleaning out your closets and donating or dumping all that stuff you never use . . . or losing 15 pounds. You're streamlining your life and traveling light!

**TIP**   Let go of anything that doesn't add value to your customer or your personal and family health and happiness.

17. Let's Make a Deal

Janis writes: Surprise! You can't do everything. Surprise! You don't have to. You can trade or outsource.

1. Trade

My husband, Mike, is an excellent editor. I wish I could get him to edit every word I write before it's published. However, he's busy with his own projects. So, I prioritize. I select the most important of my documents to be edited, observe his activities to

cipher out a task I think he might need help with (something I can do well) and create a contract. If I write out the deal cartoonishly on paper with a Sharpie, this increases the chances he'll smile and then say yes and sign on the dotted line.

Visuals lighten up the negotiations and cartoonish visuals make every conversation more fun. If you *can't* draw, your cartoons will be even funnier!

If you can't draw, your cartoons will be even funnier!

Mike had interviewed a Korean War veteran for a book he's writing and came home with two hours of the veteran's story on his phone's voice recorder. I knew the next step would be to transcribe voice to text. (Yes, there's a software for that; but it's not accurate enough.).

Transcribing isn't Mike's (or anybody's) favorite job. My offer: "I'll transcribe your recording if you'll edit my chapter of 13 pages." He accepted immediately. I won, he won, and both projects were moved expertly along!

Possible tasks you can offer to do for someone in your home:

1. Fold the laundry.
2. Proofread their copy.
3. Handle a personal business item.
4. Do the taxes.
5. Make a phone call to schedule an appointment.
6. Enter credit card splits on Quicken.
7. Rake or blow leaves.
8. _____

Ideas for tasks someone you live with (or near) could do for you:

1. Child-sit for an hour or two.
2. Get the oil changed in your car.
3. Cook a meal.
4. Proofread.
5. File papers.
6. Do an errand.
7. Cut the grass.
8. _____

2. Recruit Talent and Expertise

Sometimes we all need to face the reality that we don't have all the answers, or that our product will be much more valuable with contributions from other experts in our field. We can ask our current colleagues for help or go "outside" to people whose work we know or who come recommended by trusted  sources. Perhaps it means sharing the compensation or sharing the spotlight. We're always glad when we put away our egos and welcome talented partners.

3. Outsource

Some of us feel **we** should do everything to keep our homes spit-shiny-clean and humming without asking for help and especially without spending money to get things done. If you work from home, you're earning a certain amount of money for every hour you put in. Can you make more money doing your job or cleaning the shower? Every hour you spend vacuuming, doing laundry, and cutting the grass is an hour you aren't earning money at your job's rate. Does it make financial sense to

spend that hour earning at a higher rate and pay for a service at a lower rate? That's good decision-making.

Spend your time doing what you do best. Outsource the rest.

Which tasks at home do you not enjoy doing?

What could you be doing for your job or business if you weren't doing those tasks?

When you outsource, you're creating a job for another person; great for the economy, for your stress level, and for your loved ones who will now get to have more of your time. You (and they) are worth it!

4. Make a Deal with Yourself

If you're having trouble focusing on your work or getting started on a task you don't like, make a little deal with yourself, "When I finish this task I don't like, I get to do a fun activity." The after-work reward is your pay, just like a paycheck you receive after a week of work. You have just hired yourself and arranged a payday.

Examples of deals with yourself:

> "When I finish this report, I'll call a colleague just to catch up."

> "After completing this project, I'll book a lunch with my friend.."

> "After I talk with Kaylee's teacher, I'll go for a long walk and listen to music."

Business owner Michel Robertson rewards herself by filing all her papers away at the end of her workday, "Everything looks so neat," she says, "and sometimes I'll pick up a good steak and Prosecco for dinner."

I want something; you want something. Let's make a deal.

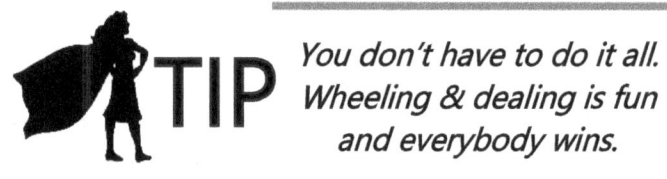

You don't have to do it all. Wheeling & dealing is fun and everybody wins.

PART FOUR:
Your Work Relationships

18. Work Remotely Without Becoming Remote

Janis writes: Working remotely, don't become "out of sight, out of mind." You don't want a cinematic fade out of your name, face, and accomplishments from the mind of your boss or colleagues. Invisibility is <u>not</u> a SuperPower.

The Four Rs

You want your boss and your colleagues or clients to

- **Recognize** – your name, your contributions and your face.

- **Reconfirm** – your project assignments, deadlines, and work specifications.

- **Remember** – your career goals and training; assignments you'd like to get.

- **Refresh** – the personal familiarity with your interests, family, and hobbies.

Call or Video with Your Manager

Schedule short *touch-base* meetings with your boss weekly. 10 minutes. Preferably video calls so she can see your face, or audio calls so she can hear your voice.

1. Cover a "recognize your progress" list:
   - Progress on your assignments
   - Projects completed (celebrate!)

2. Reconfirm:
   - Deadlines
   - Project requirements
   - Customer preferences and feedback

3. Cover your own professional development:
    o Training & assignments you'd like
    o Ask how to qualify for a promotion you'd like.

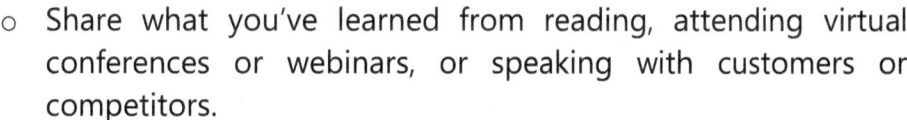

4. Ask questions to stay updated about
    o The company's direction
    o New products or services

5. Take initiative to expand your boss's horizons:
    o Share what you've learned from reading, attending virtual conferences or webinars, or speaking with customers or competitors.
    o Talk about new ideas you've thought of.

6. Refresh the relationship:
    o Ask about your boss's family, hobbies, and anything you have in common.
    o Tell one or two personal things about what's happening in your life.

7. Give positive reinforcement to your colleagues (and even your boss):
    o Sharing the credit makes you look generous and self-confident. Don't worry; it doesn't take anything away from your contributions. Quite the opposite: it shows you're a good team player who is exhibiting leadership skills.

- As soon after you know about your colleague's or boss's productive or helpful contribution, say something—don't wait (the more immediate the reinforcement, the sooner and more effectively it works).

  - Be excruciatingly specific. Not "Good job," but "Jess, your quick research helped us address the exact issues that made our customer happy."
  - Put it in writing, as well as saying it on the phone or during a video conference. With email, you can copy others who might write their own reinforcing notes to the recipient, doubling the positive impact.

- Your positive reinforcement not only increases the likelihood that the recipient will repeat that behavior, it demonstrates your willingness to share credit and leads in the creation of a more-positive work culture.*

* For more on positive reinforcement and recognition, see the book *You Made My Day*, by Janis Allen and Michael McCarthy

Stay Connected

1. Join professional organizations and attend local meetings. Volunteer for a committee to get to know individuals better.
2. Stay in touch with former colleagues and people who work for your competitors.

3. Be active in online sites in your field, as well as networking sites like Linkedin.

Here are tips from Karen Adamedes' book, *Professional in Pajamas: 101 Tips for Working from Home* that will help you "stay in mind."

1. Find out how your manager, clients, and colleagues prefer to **communicate**, and when possible, use their favorites:
   a. Text
   b. Calls
   c. Emails
   d. Meetings (in-person or virtual)

2. Use **names** at every opportunity.
   a. We all love the sound of our own names and hearing ours is sure to grab our attention.
   b. Open emails with, "Hi Jake" (or you could use the person's actual name). ☺
   c. Call people by name on calls and in virtual meetings.

3. Go to the **office** sometimes. There's nothing like showing your bright smile to keep those connections strong. Collect serendipitous information you'd have no way of knowing about if you hadn't been there in person.

Staffing Professional Brenda Smith offers some examples:

"In my current [remote working] situation we have daily "huddles" for our team to discuss the current goings-on and everyone can discuss trending subjects, issues, projects, deadlines, etc.

"Additionally, we have all-inclusive HR meetings monthly to keep everyone up to date on our corporate state of the business and global meetings every other month."

She also suggests: "Have a recognition program where you call out a colleague for going above and beyond."

 **TIP**

Let colleagues hear your voice
and see your face on a regular basis.

19. Water-Cooler Time

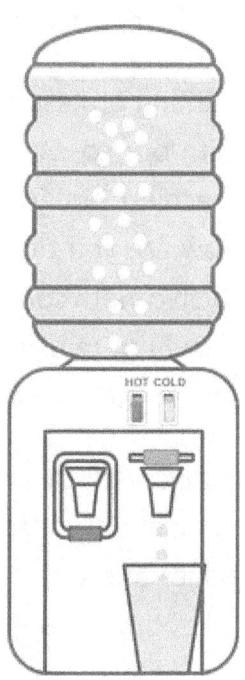

Janis writes: How can we get "water-cooler time" when there's no water cooler? Everyone has different needs for social contact. Professor Shawn McCarthy, teaching half her university classes via Zoom, said what she likes about working from home is "no social interaction." And what she dislikes is "no social interaction." Yes, both!

Jack Joyner, an IT consultant for a Fortune 50 tech company, said, "While improvements in telephony and video technology have improved immensely, I miss working in a face-to-face environment.

"Working remotely can be a challenge if your management works in an office, especially if they feel a loss of control.

"Fellow workers who don't work from home can feel envious of your situation and suspect you're not working as hard as they do. If one is undisciplined, one can fall victim to Parkinson's Law* as the time available to work is usually increased." (*Work expands to fill the time available.)

For virtual water-cooler time, text a colleague or friend to schedule a phone chat or FaceTime. Put it on your calendar. You can use these fun conversations as a self-reward for getting work done (see chapter 17. "Let's Make a Deal").

On the phone, use your wireless earbuds, put the phone in your pocket and stand up, stretch, and walk around. Keep talking as you go to the kitchen for a glass of water or cup of coffee. Mike and his longtime friend who also loves to read have formed a two-person book club. They select a book, set a date on their calendars, and discuss the book on a long, satisfying phone call.

Staffing professional Brenda Smith says, "Pick up the phone. We are in contact with our co-workers daily, but reaching out just to ask, "Hi, how are you doing?" means a lot. No work conversation, just, "Hey, I'm thinking of you and just wanted to check in."

> **Staffing professional Brenda Smith says, "Take time for yourself."**

Spouses Both Working from Home? Brenda recommends: "Take time for yourself; don't feel obligated to engage your spouse with all of your work issues and vice-versa. Ask for and make personal time, take a drive, set aside "me" time. It doesn't take much, and your spouse will most likely appreciate having his or her 'me' time.

Schedule a Break Every Day

That's five wonderful breaks each week! If you're working at home with a spouse, partner, or children, you might schedule three of these breaks per week with your family members, while reserving two days a week for your colleagues.

This builds in social or family time every day. You nurture the family relationships and the working relationships, but not in the same block of time that would have them competing for your attention, or you feeling guilty that you're spending time with one but not the other.

Gail writes: The most difficult part of working at home in the early years was having a small child that I wanted to give all my attention to every minute of the day. This meant many nights of working. I still wish I could have taken a few years off to give 100 percent.

> **No guilt is allowed for taking your social time.**

Janis writes: No guilt is allowed for taking your social time! If you're tempted to feel guilty, just think of your social time as the partial replacement for all that commuting you're <u>not</u> doing. If you're saving 60+ minutes a day by not getting into a car, bus, or train, you can un-guiltily budget at least 30 minutes during your workday for spending time with friends and family, maybe lunch. PLUS: no traffic jams, stress of getting to appointments late, or getting dressed up every day.

Do the Math

By the way, one hour a day of commute time (yours might be much more) X 5 days=5 hours per week X 50 weeks=250. **250 hours** per year to play with! Literally play. Go for it with gusto and without guilt!

You might be an introvert who needs alone time to re-charge and avoids water-cooler chat at all cost. If so, take back some of that "I'm-not-commuting-any-more" time for reading, napping, walking, or staring into space.

Get out of your house at least once a day. Meet other people for business or just friends having coffee. Or just go outside.

- Take a walk.
- Get some groceries.
- Pick up Chinese.
- Tour your hometown museum.
- Browse in a shop.
- Drop into your town's visitor center and grab some brochures.
- Sit down in the public library and read a magazine that you'd never buy.
- Walk into the county courthouse just to look around at the architecture and art and be happy you're not there as a defendant.

These can become micro-vacations that make you a tourist in your hometown and give your brain a little break!

TIP If you don't feel like interacting with people, go outside and enjoy your surroundings.

20. Make Friends with Your Delivery Drivers

Janis writes: Everyone is now receiving more deliveries to our homes than ever. All those years we were at an office or factory during the day, we never had the pleasure of meeting the people who left goodies on our porches. Now we can run to the door when we see or hear their trucks and say hi. We learned that Eric Rasheed (pictured above), our UPS driver, likes eggnog. One cold December day, we invited him inside to have a mug with us. We learned about his son, the football player. It's now a bright spot in our day when we see his big brown truck with his friendly face smiling at us.

Introduce Yourself

It's a perfect way to have a few seconds of contact with another human being during a full day of staying home. Ask your driver for his or her name and use it every time she or he approaches. Fling your front door open and greet your drivers with a big smile. Thank them for their work. Offer them a bottle of water.

Many work-from-homers say the only thing they miss about not going to the office is social interactions. Even though your delivery persons may only have a quick pause as they jog back to their trucks, their familiar faces can brighten one minute of your day.

Gail writes: My friendship with my UPS driver developed with multiple conversations about an exotic carved lizard I had to return several times. (Don't ask.) During our conversations, I learned that he was taking piano lessons, something he had wanted to do since childhood. After that, I occasionally asked, "How are the piano lessons going?" and enjoyed his updates. One can make friends without even leaving the house!

 **TIP**   **Introduce yourself to your delivery drivers and make friends with them.**

PART FIVE:
SHARPEN THE SAW—YOU!

21. Exercise. Give Your Brain a Break and a Boost.

Janis writes: A former colleague said, "I never eat breakfast—only four cups of coffee—skip lunch, and reward myself with a nice big dinner because I don't deserve to eat until I've accomplished something." So she spent the day being impatient and crabby with people around her and carried 40 extra pounds (eating huge meals just before bed).

You may have been too self-conscious to exercise when you worked in an office—now's your big chance! No one will see you stretching and straining at home except your cat, and she doesn't care.

According to Get-Fit Guy Brock Armstrong, writing in *Scientific American* December 26, 2018, "Exercise affects the brain in many ways. It increases heart rate, which pumps more oxygen to the brain . . . Exercise also promotes brain plasticity by stimulating growth of new connections between cells in many important cortical areas of the brain."

How about short-term: helping you solve that customer complaint this afternoon?

According to technology consultant and author of the book *The New How*, Nilofer Merchant, "Research has found that exercising on a regular basis, especially walking or some other type of aerobic exercise, can help foster creativity. Walking meetings not only liberate the butt, they liberate the creative juices."

Gail writes: Exercise whenever possible on home equipment or take a walk. Also, go outside and soak up some vitamin-D rays when you can, which is another plus of working from home. During the summer, I take a break to work in the yard while listening to music: fun and getting something done. Looking at nature is the best mental exercise of all. You can always gaze at the sky.

Janis writes: On the following page, fitness trainer Bill Bailey shares quick tips for stretching and developing strength at home, between video conferences, phone calls, and long stretches of sitting and deep concentration. Bailey is certified with the National Academy of Sports Medicine and the National Council on Strength and Conditioning. For more info about virtual workouts: bbailey@reagan.com

Consult your doctor before beginning any exercise program. The authors and publisher are not responsible for injury resulting from exercise.

5 Easy Exercises for Stretching, Strength, and Balance

Start the day with these or intersperse one every hour or two:

1. **Sitting or Standing Tall with Extended Posture**: Hold arms straight up as if signaling "Touchdown!" Slowly pulse your arms 2 inches toward the back for 10-15 seconds. (Didn't you always want to call a touchdown?)

2. **Shoulder and Neck Stretches**: For 5-10 seconds several times a day, slowly and gently do the following:
   a. Tip your head down toward your chest.
   b. Tip your head left to right.
   c. Roll your head in a circle, clockwise.
   d. Roll your head in a circle, counterclockwise.

3. **Single Leg Balancing**: While holding onto a counter or high table, bend one knee slightly, raising that foot off the floor. Shift all your weight onto the other foot, leaning into that heel for stability. Hold 10-30 seconds. Repeat with other leg.

4. **Hip, Glute, and Lower-Back Stretches**: Lying on your back, pull one knee up and across toward the opposite shoulder. Hold this stretch 10-20 seconds or longer. Repeat with other knee.

5. **Cat and Cow**: You know this one. The Cow: Kneel on a mat or rug and put palms flat, "all fours" position. Keep your head in a straight line with your body so you're looking at the floor. Slowly allow your back to sag. Next, do the Cat: Keep your back relaxed as you lift your face toward the ceiling. Then round your back up at the waist as far as you can by contracting your lower abdominal muscles as you lower the top of your head toward the floor. Purrrrrrrrrrrr!

Also, remember those yoga positions you practiced at all those classes over the years? Namaste.

Focusing your body's reactions to movement pushes business thoughts out for a few minutes and gives you a little vacation of the mind.

Don't Get Comfy Yet

Here's how some more work-from-homers get exercise during their workdays.

Harry Halmshaw, a university professor teaching from home with Zoom, describes his working-from-home habits:

"I alternate sitting and standing. I sit while teaching my Zoom classes, then stand to do any online work and recording lecture videos. I use a fold-up table, then wheel in a kitchen work island, which happens to be just the right height and size for standing and working with my laptop. Even in sneakers, feet need a soft surface if you'll be standing for hours. I use an exercise mat that I already had at home.

"Aside from doing a typical workout at the beginning or end of my day, I stop working at my desk throughout the day to do small chunks of exercise. One day, I might do 10 air squats every time I walk into another room. So, by the end of the day, I might have done a hundred or hundreds. Then the next day, I'll do something different, an upper-body exercise, perhaps. Alternatively, mix these up on the same day to get an all-over workout in one day. This is the 'Greasing the Groove' technique whereby you stop to do short sets of any exercise throughout your day."

> **Every time you walk into another room, do a short set of exercises.**

Can't stand the thought of exercising for a full hour? The prof's idea of doing some type of exercise every time you cross into a different room is a good way to build in a visual reminder to work your body. Put a sticky note reading EXERCISE or SQUATS on your door frames for the first week or two. Soon you'll be automatically exercising when you pass through a doorway.

Professor Shawn McCarthy, teaching virtual classes from home, also uses the standing position to get her body into a different position. To elevate her computer, she slips a shoebox underneath and a yoga block beside it to place her mouse at the higher level. Again, use the "found" items you already have handy.

Brenda Smith, a staffing company professional, advises "Maintain your normal routine; if you used to get up and work out prior to heading to the office, keep doing that. After work, again keep doing it.

"Add exercise to your daily meetings: If you are not on a video call, move your chair and step, step, step! You can do leg lifts, arm toning, all sorts of movements to burn calories during those not-so-exciting meetings!

"Invest in a small cycling product that fits under your desk; (most are inexpensive, starting at under $40). You can peddle as you sit answering emails, talking on the phone, visual meetings, etc.

"To make exercise inclusive in your daily routine, if possible, have your printer, stapler, daily projects on the other side of the room so you must get up and move."

Michel Robertson, an officer of a non-profit board, says, "It's so easy to get absorbed in my work and forget to exercise. All of a sudden, it's time for dinner or the evening news. So, I schedule my virtual workouts with a trainer. Having an appointment makes me more likely to do it."

Consulting IT specialist Jack Joyner gets up from his desk every 15-20 minutes to stretch, breathe deeply, and walk around. "One of my favorite 'hacks' for conference calls is to use a good, wireless headset and pace during calls," he says. "You'd be amazed how many steps you can add to your daily count during that one-hour-was-this-really-necessary mass meeting. (Just be sure you mute your mic when you go to the restroom.)"

Gail writes: The importance of hitting the mike mute was emphasized to me during an international conference call. I was merely listening in and recording the conversation for an article about the client. Suddenly the very distinct British accent of one of the participants said of the client, "This fellow sounds like a complete ass!" Then, "Oh my gosh! Is my mike on?" This was followed

by quite a pause and somehow the consultant in charge managed to move the conversation along. When I transcribed the conversation, I could hear the very faint sound of my self-muffled snickering.

Advertising Plus owner Kathy Peterson sets an alarm that goes off every hour to signal her to get up and walk around and stretch. [I found four free apps for Androids and three in the Apple store. Just type in "stretch reminder."] "Also," Kathy said, "I pump my feet a lot when I'm sitting, to help circulation."

Deskercise: The Swivel. This is a fun one. Marketing manager Jeannie Krill writes on Hubspot/blog:

https://blog.hubspot.com/marketing/benefits-of-exercise-on-creativity

"Keep your back straight, put your fingertips on the edge of your desk, lift your feet up, and twist your chair from side to side. It's good for your core —all you need is a swiveling desk chair."

Walking dates with a friend keep me honest. Knowing that my buddy will be showing up at a certain time and place is effective accountability. Sometimes at 10:00 AM and sometimes at 3:00 PM. Both those are great times to give my brain a little vacation.

Mike sometimes uses a stand-up desk so he can shift his feet back and forth. [If you do stand a lot, consider an anti-fatigue mat. Those made for kitchens are less expensive than those made for offices—under $30.00.]

Go Soak Your Head!
Get Your Eyeballs Away from that Screen.

Associate pastor and former public policy researcher Eric Torrence writes in THINDIFFERENCE.COM:

"Time and time again, I find my best ideas come in the shower. If a problem has been bugging me throughout the day, or if I lack inspiration, a shower almost always helps. I know I'm not the only one. Cognitive scientist Scott Barry Kaufman did a study that found 72% of people get creative ideas in this particular location. He said, 'We did a multinational study and found that people reported more creative inspiration in their showers than they did at work.'

"Why is this the case? Showers are a safe place that provide 'a dopamine high, relaxed state, and distracted mind,' factors that are ideal for creativity and idea formation."

https://www.thindifference.com/2018/01/best-ideas-come-shower/#:~:text=Why%20is%20this%20the%20case,and%20yes%2C%20taking%20a%20shower

The shower may be one of the few places we can go during the workday where our eyes aren't on a screen.

Additional ways to avoid looking at a screen:

- Listen to calming music with your eyes closed.

- Go outside and study the color, texture, and shape of a leaf. See if you can sketch it when you get back inside.

- Eat lunch at a place where you can look out a window, leaving all screens in another room.

- Take a walk without your phone.

- Stare at the sky. Imagine shapes from clouds like you did as a kid.

As Eric Torrence concludes in his article: "You might be just one shower away from your next great idea!"

TIP

"Keep the juices flowing by jangling around gently as you move." ~ Satchel Paige

22. Sleep

Janis writes: When you can't drift off at night, you have the option (since you're working from home) to go to your desk and do some work. Perhaps thinking of work is keeping you awake: "Will I remember to do (whatever) tomorrow?" You can do it now, at midnight, or make ready (write it down on your bedside notepad) to stop it from nagging away at your too-alert brain.

If you just can't sleep for other reasons (full of streaming ideas for your current project, worries over a work or personal encounter), you can still make use of the hour it will take for you to become sleepy again by getting a head start on tomorrow. With your computer or work documents just a few steps away, you can unburden your brain and use your time for something other than tossing and turning.

How Much Sleep is Enough for You?

My dad worked two jobs, six days a week, for his 42-year working career. His main job was as second shift (2:30 to 10:30 PM) spinning-room supervisor in a textile mill. But every morning he was out by 6:30 AM building spec houses to sell. He took a shower/rest/lunch break at 11:30 and started answering phone calls around 1:00 PM from employees who were sick and couldn't come in to

> **"Every hour of sleep before midnight counts double." –G.E. Allen**

work. He told me, "If I live to be 90, I surely won't sleep 30 of those years. Eight hours of sleep would be a third of my life. I won't do it." He got by on six hours. When we were later-than-usual going to bed, my mother would say, "We'll have to sleep fast tonight."

- How many hours of sleep do you need? Your life experience tells you.
- What is your optimum time to go to bed for the best "all-night-through" sleep?
- Are you a night owl or a morning lark?
- Give yourself permission to nap if you feel more productive after a few winks (10 to 30 minutes max).

7 Tips for Sleeping Better and More
1. Get some natural sunlight during the day.
2. Exercise.
3. Make your room dark. Blackout curtains can be a good investment.
4. Make the temperature work for you. Many experts recommend a cooler room.
5. Use comfortable earplugs if noise is an issue.

6. Eat lightly in the evening to avoid the discomfort of a full tummy and the cranking up of your digestive system to deal with all that food in the hopper.

7. Read something unrelated to your work. Get your mind into a good novel to push out your to-do list at bedtime.

Sleep is restorative to our brains and creativity as well as our bodies. "Sleep on it" is wise advice for any decision we're not ready to make, or any emotion that's taking too much of our energy. You've probably had the happy experience of waking up with the perfect solution to a problem in your head, seemingly coming from nowhere.

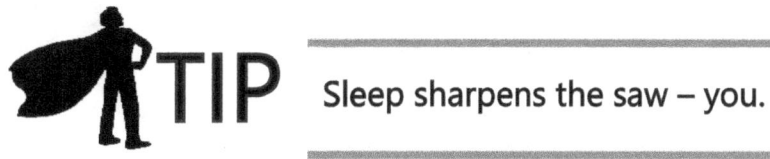

Sleep sharpens the saw – you.

23. Power Napping

Janis writes: "As wartime prime minister of Britain, Sir Winston Churchill always went to bed for at least an hour as early as possible in the afternoon, postponing cabinet meetings so that he could enter the ancient sleepability gate as soon as it opened." (From the book *Winston Churchill's Afternoon Nap* by Jeremy Campbell)

Imagine having a lie-down while leading the charge to defeat Hitler and save Western civilization. He even changed into pajamas. Now that's a serious nap!

If you're a power napper, you're in good company! You don't have to hide it anymore. You work from home; napping is your SuperPower.

Nap Like a Soldier

From *Reader's Digest*, March 2021: "Uncle Sam wants you—to take a nap! The U.S. Army recently rolled out new guidelines that encourage soldiers to take 'short, infrequent naps to restore wakefulness and promote performance.' This is from the Army's *Field Manual FM-722 Holistic Health and Fitness*."

Know Thyself

Are you a Power Napper or a ProcrastiNapper? Are you more productive or less productive after a nap? Let's find out.

What's your history?

a. After a 3:00 PM nap, have you usually gone back to work before 4:00 PM with renewed interest and enthusiasm, and completed an item on your to-do list? You're a Power Napper.

b. Have you usually groggily dragged yourself from one horizontal surface (bed, perhaps) to another (sofa, perhaps), where you remained for the balance of that day? You might be a ProcrastiNapper.

Power napper, or ProcrastiNapper?

If your answer is Power Napper, you're using that brief sleep to re-charge and rejuvenate your energy and creativity. It's a good investment. As Stephen Covey, author of *The Seven Habits of Highly Successful People* wrote, "Take time to sharpen your saw."

If you must admit that you've usually been a ProcrastiNapper, don't despair. You can still become a Power Napper with these diagnostics and prescriptions:

1. How long are your naps? Most Power Nappers find that very short naps (10 to 30 minutes) refresh them, while long naps (more than a half-hour) lull them into deeper sleep that's harder to shake off.
2. If you're groggy and lethargic after your nap, set an alarm to shorten it. Start with 30 minutes. If it takes you 5-10 minutes to fall asleep, you still have 20 minutes in dreamland.
3. Experiment to find your Goldilocks ("just right") time for napping.
4. When your usual, post-nap behavior is to go back to work and produce something, you're officially a Power Napper.

Tips for Great Power Napping: QCD (Quiet, Cool, Dark)

1. Find the place in your home with the smallest likelihood for noise and interruptions.
2. Turn off all noise-making devices: phone, computer, any electronics that screech or squeal.
3. Let your family members know you're napping from (name a time) to (name a time) and are not to be disturbed. I have a little tent-card sign (shown at right) that I put in a place where my husband will see it.
4. Darken the room or wear a mask. I sleep best in a dark, cool place where I can close the curtains. (My husband says I'm a bat.)

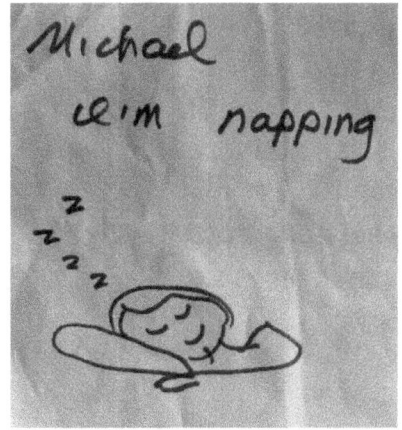

5. Adjust your clothes to be most comfortable and take off your shoes if that helps.

6. Count backward from 100 to help you fall asleep if needed.

Micro-Napping

Some real Power Nappers can simply put their heads down on their desks (remember grade school?) or lean back in their chairs for tiny snoozes. I envy you if you're one of those lucky dozers.

Feel Too Guilty to Sleep During the Workday?

Someone said she could never take a nap because she remembers how her mother took an hour nap EVERY day when she was growing up, and she thought that was a lazy, wasteful, and selfish habit. She said, "She even changed into pajamas. It was horrible!" This friend will probably never be able to enjoy a quick, refreshing snooze during daylight hours. In her opinion, napping is synonymous with laziness. So sorry.

Power Napping is not for everyone, even people who work from home. Yet, it is one tool for productivity and pleasure. And it's FREE.

Power napping is free!

Home designer Stephen Jackson said, "I have practiced and been a proponent of power naps for over 40 years. I can lie down for 20 minutes around 2:00 every afternoon, and without an alarm clock, awake refreshed and ready to conquer the world!"

I'm a Power Napper and That's OK

See how popular napping is? Here's proof with all the words invented to describe it!

- Catch some Zs
- Slumber
- Crash
- Snooze
- Catnap
- Shuteye
- Siesta
- Forty winks
- Drowse
- Nod off
- Resting my eyes
- Somnolent
- Study the inside of my eyelids for a bit
- Be in the arms of Morpheus (the Greek god of sleep)

TIP

Just say you're
"resting your eyes."

SECTION THREE: DEFENDING YOUR WORKSPACE AGAINST INVADERS

24. "THEY KNOW I'M HERE!"

Gail writes: No, this isn't a script for an episode of *The Walking Dead*. We don't fear zombies, we fear the walking Favor-Demanders and the telephonic Errand-Askers. "Since you work from home, would you do me a favor?" "Since you work from home, would you check my porch every hour for a delivery?" We fear the dreaded words: "Since you work from home . . . "

The Dreaded Words:

"Since you work from home..."

People often think because you work from home, you really have no deadlines or obligations. They're the first to ask you to do "favors." "Well, you don't have to go into work like /do," the favor-askers remark. What?! For years, I was the only person arranging my work around taking my mother to appointments—and still getting my work completed on time.

- I was asked to drive my sister's elderly mother-in-law's cat to the vet. I did.
- I spent a whole day in the ER with my next-door neighbor who was suffering from severe migraine. Her husband had called me and said he couldn't get away. I later found out he was golfing!
- My neighbor called begging me to help her to look for her lost dog. She insisted on driving but was so frantic she ran over a neighbor's mailbox. We left a note and yes, we found the dog.
- In high school, my son David's friend called frantically: "Miss Gail, Miss Gail. I missed my bus. Mom will kill me! She's at work. Can you come and take me to school?!" Geez! *Yes, I got him to school on time.*
- I was asked to have kids dropped off early at my home so their parents could get to work and then, of course, take them and pick them up from school. *I did so for an entire school year.*

Help! They know I'm here! There's more, but I shan't go on. Oh, I might add, no snow days when working from home! Well, maybe I will go on.

And I don't even get a snow day!

Often, if you work from home and have a telephone appointment for an interview or meeting, people blow you off. No worries (for them) that you've planned your schedule around the appointment. The unspoken message I got from such inconsideration was, "You've got time to waste. What else have you got to do . . . home worker!" 😊   (Studies show that people who work from home get a lot more done.)

Speaking of social contact, that's a double-edged sword even if you lean toward introversion, which I do. My behaviors over the years have ranged from hiding like Boo Radley* against the wall when someone came to the door, to going to the grocery store just to see other humans. (I often call them "the others.") *Boo Radley was the reclusive neighbor few people ever saw in the novel *To Kill A Mockingbird*, by Harper Lee.

From *Secrets of the Remote Workforce* by Teresa Douglas, Holly Gordon, and Mike Webber:

> "No one really understands what other people [who work from home] do for work. The home is a place of rest. It's where you raise your family, where you do your chores on weekends, where you watch TV and relax. Adding business to the mix, even if you have a designated office area to work from, complicates things. Others have a hard time understanding where the line between work and non-work is. Fortunately, the trick to navigating these conversations is straightforward: Anticipate questions and comments and take preemptive action, or at least be prepared to respond to the usual queries and misconceptions."

 Mike writes: Castles from the Middle Ages had two lines of defense: outer and inner. The outer was a wall surrounded by a moat. If the outer wall was breached by the enemy, the defenders retreated behind an inner wall, sometimes a tower known as the *castle keep* (as in: "Keep Out!"). So far, we have discussed guerilla tactics and skills for defending your inner wall from encroachers from within: roommates, children, spouses, partners and the odd zombie from your basement.

Now it's time to discuss defense of your outer wall against encroachers from without: neighbors, in-laws, parents, siblings, sellers of band candy or cookies, friends and evangelical doorbell-ringers. You met Janis' cousin Dot in chapter 12. Dot has the perfect outer defense sign beside her front door (pictured at right).

Or you could create a "Work Hours" sign that you hang on your front doorknob during your working hours, like the one below.

Work Hours:
8-12pm. 1-5pm.

From 12-1pm or after 5pm the PIN code is: "I've brought you a cake, pie or casserole."

If you make the mistake of opening the door or answering the phone, your fallback defense is, "I'm working. What can I do for you?" If they still have the chutzpah* to ask you for a favor or errand, your next line of defense is, "Sorry, I'm working now."

*Leo Rosten's book *The Joys of Yiddish* defines chutzpah: Like the defendant convicted of killing his parents, who then asked for leniency on the grounds that he was an orphan!

If they persist, don't make the fateful 2nd order mistake: *giving a reason why not.* You don't have to give a reason why not. Giving a reason often provokes the generic counterattack: "Here's why my request is more important than your reason why not," or, "You can always do that later. I need this NOW."

Your second line of defense is called "broken record"—repeat after anything they say: "No. I'm working now." If that doesn't work after three repetitions, go nuclear, go to the Dot Allen doomsday weapon, "BYE."

Resist the invaders! Defend your time and your space.

**TIP**   **You don't have to give a reason why not.**

25. Passport Entry

Once upon a time, in an office tower far far away, people Worked in Cubicles.

Mike writes: **Remember cubicles?** It was like working out of the cardboard box your new refrigerator came in. Cramped, but cozy. Tiny, but with some privacy. At least your office mates didn't pile dirty dishes in your cubicle. Cubicle walls screened out visual distractions. And partially screened some noise distractions, like the muffled hacking cough of that annoying person three cubicles down WHO REFUSED TO USE COUGH DROPS!

Cubicles, we now fondly remember, did not have children randomly interrupting and demanding "TELL FREDDIE TO STOP LOOKING AT ME!" Cubicles did not have office mates sitting down with their phones and talking forever IN LOUD CELL PHONE VOICES, did not have spouses asking abruptly "HAVE YOU SEEN MY COFFEE CUP?" Your cubicle was your semi-castle.

Now that you have claimed your at-home workspace and marked the perimeters with **Work Scene**™ tape, you are ready for the next phase of Work From Home super-power-dom: **Defending** your work space against encroachers, interrupters, invaders, and demanders (yes, that includes nosy neighbors).

Encroachers, interrupters, and demanders are all the minions of the evil super-villain **Dr. Distracto**, whose distracting tentacles doom deadlines daily. Learn to recognize these tentacles of Dr. Distracto, reaching out to seize your attention and make you miss your deadlines, cleverly disguised as:

DR. DISTRACTO

- "May I sit here and read my magazine?" The warm body in your workspace Encroacher. Before long, he says "Listen to this! It says here . . ." Don't be fooled! The **Encroacher** is a *dreaded tentacle of distraction!*

- "Mommy (Daddy) would you button my coat for me?" "Honey, have you seen my briefcase?" The small request that pulls you into the Timeless Temple of Doom. You end up asking, "Wow! Where did the morning go?" The *Demander* is another *dreaded tentacle of distraction.*

- "May I interrupt you for a moment? Would you take a minute and edit this for me?" The wily *Interrupter* wants just a minute . . . that turns into 30.

In the Middle Ages in Europe, villagers, farmers and merchants faced the constant threat of encroachers, demanders, and interrupters who wanted their food, their wives, their children, and their stuff. Their solution? Castles, not cubicles! Make your WorkSpace your CASTLE. Defend it!

How to Keep Encroachers Out

Defend your castle boundaries with these super-powers:

- Passports required for entry
- Posted Hours for requests & interruptions (Make your schedule visible.)
- Response cost (Charge for your time.)
- Nyet, no, non, not now. (Dr. No is actually a good guy.)

Post a homemade sign requiring a passport for entry into your workspace. Then create your own passport for your *"Republic of WorkSpace."*

Make the passport

- Have Requirements to obtain it
- Have an expiration + renewable date/time
- Contain a list of requirements for entry
- Spell out days/times when it may be used

Passport for the Republic of Work-Space-Opia

Name: _____

WFH citizenship:

- Dad _____
- Mom _____
- Child _____
- Roommate_____
- Neighbor_____
- Other _____

This Passport is valid (renews daily) because
I have performed the following duties of citizenship:

1. Homework _____
2. My laundry _____
3. Dried & put away dishes _____
4. Swept or vacuumed _____
5. Set up coffee for tomorrow morning _____
6. Cleaned my room _____
7. Made up my bed _____
8. Put away my toys _____
9. Mowed lawn or took out trash _____
10. Other: _____

When all requirements for validity are signed off, this Passport is valid for a one-day entry into the Sovereign WorkSpace during these times:

_____am to _____am

_____pm to _____pm

_____pm to _____pm

Posted Hours

Retail shops and post offices have posted hours. So should you. Shopkeepers need time to stock shelves and clean the shop without interruption. It is part of their work. You also need uninterrupted chunks of time to get your work done. So decide on your "hours of operation," write or type them on a sheet of paper, post them and announce them at a family/roommate/partner meeting.

It might look like this:

WorkSpace Hours

9am – 12pm   1pm-5pm

Kindly schedule all requests and interruptions before or after these hours of operation. Note: Up-to-date passport required for entry.

Charge for Your Time

When I go to the post office to mail a package, they tell me "You'll have to fill out this form first." When I go to the UPS Store to send a package, they ask "Where is it going?" Then they do the rest. Guess which one I'm more likely to go to? You guessed it! The UPS store. Whenever there is a "You'll have to . . ." involved, that is a *response cost.* I have to do something before they will do anything for me. If the response cost is too high, I do it less or I go elsewhere.

The passport process automatically imposes a response cost. Homework, dishes, etc. However, if you choose not to use the passport method, you can still charge a response cost. You just have to get into the habit.

"Before I check your homework, *you'll have to* load and start the dishwasher."

"Before I go look for your lost briefcase, *you'll have to* take these letters to the mailbox."

"Before I copy-edit your latest chapter, *you'll have to* plant this hydrangea for me."

Mom's Office

Don't come in unless you want chores.

What are the benefits of "You'll have to"?

- They'll think twice before interrupting you.
- They'll ask themselves "Is it easier to do it myself?"
- They'll interrupt less and make fewer requests.
- They learn how to do it themselves; (self-sufficiency = self-confidence).
- You get stuff done from your own "things to do" list.

Nyet, no, non, not now. (Dr. No is actually a good guy.)

This super-power takes courage. Why? Because we think people who say "no" are unlikable. We all want to be liked. So, we all say "yes" at times when we really want to say "no." Or worse, we say "yes" or "maybe" and then don't do it. Now we'll be seen as unreliable and a person who does not keep his or her word.

Here's how to summon courage. Say "yes" to yourself first. In Stephen Covey's book *The 7 Habits of Highly Effective People*, he advises us to say yes to our own projects and family time first. How? By blocking out chunks of time for them in our calendars. Then when someone asks us to do something, we look in our calendars or planners, see that the time is blocked off to do our own work projects, and say "No. Sorry, I have other time commitments right now."

Then don't give in. You have to teach others (and yourself) that "no" means no.

**TIP** After you post your hours, stick to them.

26. Interrupt Interruptions: Yes You Can.

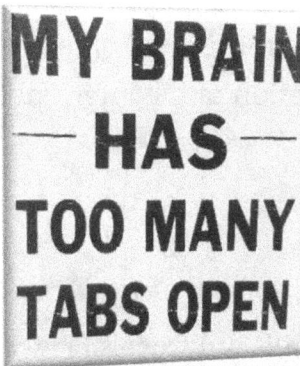

Janis writes: Interruptions are a part of life: can't live with 'em, can't live without 'em. If we didn't have interruptions, we'd be dead. For some people, "If I didn't have interruptions, I wouldn't have a job." Interruptions bring us customers, social contact, intellectual stimulation, and sometimes hugs from little ones—many good things. They also bring breaks in our concentration, delays in getting our work done, wasted time, annoyance, and sometimes increase other people's dependence on us for our help.

People lament, "I get so many interruptions!" I believe them. I also believe that we can control up to 80% of the disruption they insert into our workflow. That other 20% that we can't or don't want to avoid are emergencies involving our loved ones, last-minute changes by a customer or that important call you've been waiting for.

My assertion that we can "control" 80% of interruptions means that you have the ability to

- delay the intrusion until a later time when you <u>want</u> to focus on that topic or person;
- re-direct the interrupter to a different source for help or attention;
- shorten the duration of the interruption by at least 80%.

Interruptions by People

Evaluate each interruption: you either want it or you don't want it. If you want it because you like spending time with that person, relax and enjoy. If you're happy to use your time training, mentoring, or coaching a co-worker, go for it.

If it's an interruption that you don't welcome because it's not productive for you or reinforces non-productive habits of others, don't encourage the behavior by giving attention to it. That's reinforcing an undesired behavior, and you know that **anything you reinforce, you'll get more of.**

Use the tips below to
- shorten the amount of time you spend on that interruption;
- reduce the likelihood of that person interrupting you in the future.

Tips for Reducing Interruptions: Duration & Frequency

1. **Minimize the duration of the in-person interruption.**
   a. Say, "Sorry, I have to focus on this deadline."

   b. When someone enters your workspace, immediately stand. They'll ask you for something. As you answer, begin walking away from your workspace. They'll walk with you, because your attention is what they came for. While you're walking, re-direct their request.

2. **Re-direct.**
   a. Give a brief answer if you can do it in 30 seconds or less. Smile and say, "I'm getting back to my project." Make a U-turn and go back to your workspace. (You're re-directing your physical presence in this example.)

   b. Re-direct their request to another source. If you can't help them in 30 seconds, suggest an alternate source they can use:
      - Internet search
      - Another person

- Themselves. "Use the same process you used for last week's project. Let me know how it's going," or "Go ahead and get started. Let me know if you get stuck."

c. Re-direct the content of their talk if it's non-productive. For instance, whining, gossip, complaining, off-task details you have no interest in hearing; or anything that's wasting your time.

- Interrupt mid-sentence (before they get more than five seconds of your attention, which is what they want) with, "What's the status of your market research?" or "How are you coming along on your science project?"

- If they make that U-turn and "go with you" to the more productive topic, make a brief positive comment to reinforce that talk, "Good idea!"

See how you're not ignoring the person; you're ignoring the negative talk. As soon as the talk becomes positive, give your attention. You can switch from "stop" to "go" in a split-second to reinforce behaviors you want.

- Then make your own U-turn with, "Great. I'm on a deadline. See you later." Again, re-direct <u>your</u> physical presence to the place you want to be—at work.

- Don't wait for the full explanation of the reason for the interruption (listening is reinforcing the talk). Nip it in the bud with clear and assertive cues for a different behavior. Say something like, "Try this . . ." As soon as you see that behavior, lay on the reinforcement. "See how that works?" That behavior will increase in the future.

If you want to give your child help with homework, get her to do some of it. Then reinforce her after she's completed part of her task:

"OK, you work on it until 12:15. We'll stop for lunch and I'll help you."

"Get started with what you know, and I'll help you at 2:30."

3. **Signal You're "Closed."**

A great idea from Karen Adamedes in her book, *Professionals in Pajamas.* "Wear headphones. You don't have to be listening to anything." Point to your headphones and look at your screen. Don't look up again.

4. Post your OPEN times like a storekeeper.

OPEN for questions from 10:25 to 10:40

Gail writes: Once upon a time I read an article saying that prolonged staring at a computer screen could cause eye damage and that even wearing sunglasses could be protective. Ever the adventuress, I grabbed a pair of sunglasses from a junk drawer—cobalt blue, rubber rims, John-Lennon round. "Oh, an earpiece is missing; no matter. I'm just staring at a computer screen."

Then, as I took a break and decided to put on some Pink Floyd music, the doorbell rang. It was a group of religious folks. I answered the door, greeted them, and accepted their pamphlet. With "Dark Side of the Moon" blaring in the background, they somewhat timidly asked if I wanted to pray.

I had forgotten about my lopsided, almost fluorescent glasses at this point and replied enthusiastically, "Sure!" It was the shortest prayer I've ever heard and with a quick "Amen" they turned and scurried, almost ran, away. I thought, "I wonder what happened to them. They even forgot to ask for a donation. I would have given them one." Moral: It's true. You can re-direct people in many ways . . . sometimes, even without trying.

Heads Down

Business owner Kristen McKenzie reserves "heads down" time to focus. She describes it, "Heads down time, to me, is focus time. Ideally, it's not disturbed, but it's time I might dedicate to thinking about a problem or working solo on a specific project."

 **TIP**

Re-direct interruptions.

A King or Queen's workspace is his or her castle.

The treasure inside is your time, your Majesty!

Defend it.

27. Dr. No Is Your Friend

Mike writes: In the first James Bond film, the villain was known as Dr. No. In one company I worked for, the CFO's middle nickname was No. Tony "No" Jenkins. His job was to say no to new expenditures. People who say no have a negative reputation. We, therefore, dislike being the person who says "No."

Gail adds: Over the years, I seldom went out to lunch, because I couldn't quit thinking of the work time I was losing. I usually just told people, "I'd love to meet you, but I just have too much to do." They understood.

Accountability Services owner Michel Robertson said, "It's difficult for me to turn down a request because my personality is that of a rescuer. The technique I learned in business was to

1. acknowledge the other person's need;
2. explain why I cannot help;
3. suggest an alternative source for help"

How to Say No Without Even Using the Word

- "I'm not the best resource to help with this."
- "My time is all spoken for."
- "Let me know how you handle that."
- "I know you can do it."
- "I'm on a deadline."

You Don't Have to Justify "No"

No "good" reason need be offered for saying no (for example: a prior commitment, someone else needs me for something, can't afford it, etc.). Just the very fact that you want to say "No" is the only reason you need to say it. In fact, the same is true for any behavior someone else wants you to do, such as the following:

- Buying cookies or band candy
- Eating food someone offers
- Joining an organization
- Attending a fundraiser (or working the event)
- Leaving an event without staying to the bitter end
- Contributing to charities, large or small

Practice saying "No" today with anybody who asks you to stop what you're doing and do what they want you to do.

"No" is one of the most difficult yet liberating words in any language.
—Mark Helprin, Claremont Review of Books

 28. "And Stay Out!"

G ail writes: My four-year-old son (now grown), David was told to go to his room for some misbehavior. He dutifully went in, slammed the door in his parents' faces as they stood in the hallway, and shouted, "And stay out!" 😊 Young David was defending his castle.

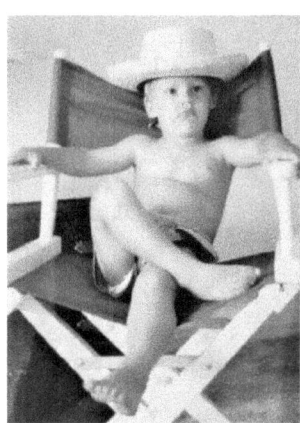

Janis writes: The rule of thumb with children is

If you don't find something for children to do, they'll find something for you to do.

David the Director

Games and puzzles and Legos are things that they can enjoy for hours. But as a parent, you already know this!

What tasks can you challenge your kids to do? Below are some ideas to teach and coach your kids to do. Give them a hug, a checkmark, or sticker, and LOTS of positive reinforcement.

Kids' Chores

Age-by-Age Checklist from American Academy of Child & Adolescent Psychiatry* (cited in *REAL SIMPLE* magazine, August 2020, page 72)

- 2 to 3 years old: Put toys away and dress themselves without help
- 4 to 5 years old: Help feed pets, make their beds (not perfectly, of course), and help clear the table after breakfast, lunch, and dinner
- 6 to 7 years old: Wipe tables and counters, put laundry away, and sweep floors
- 7 to 9 years old: Load and unload the dishwasher, help with meal preparation, and pack their own lunches for school
- 10 to 11 years old: Change their sheets and clean the kitchen and bathroom
- 12 and above: Wash the car and help with younger siblings

Make a Game of Getting Stuff Done

Families who play together stay together—especially those who make work into play! Erasable boards and "Good for Me" charts (online for about $20.00, including marking pens) are all you need to create fun to-do lists, visual feedback, and prompts/reminders to give positive reinforcement. A good variety of charts and kits can be found at www.lakeshorelearning.com. Or you can make your own!

This simple system can replace all manner of nagging, frustration, resentment, and complaints: "I have to do everything around here," or "There's nothing to do around here."

1. Involve your kids or let them design the whole chart with colored markers, borders, and stickers you can find in the school supplies aisle, office supply aisles in big box stores, or online.

2. Kids can have fun teasing Mom and Dad by writing in chores for them too!

3. Anything that has fun and teasing involved immediately "loses weight," meaning that the heaviness of "have to do, hate to do, nag to get done" dissipates and the whole project becomes lighter.

Our daughter Shawn earned money as shown; she wasn't just *given* an allowance.

GOOD FOR SHAWN								
	Mon	Tue	Wed	Thur	Fri	Sat	Sun	Total
Homework ($1.00)	√	√	√	√	√		√	$6.00
Set table ($0.10)	√	√	√	√	√			$0.50
Clear table ($0.25)	√	√	√	√	√			$1.25
Dust 1 room ($0.50)			√					$0.50
Do laundry ($0.50)				√				$0.50
Cut front-yard grass ($5.00)						√		$5.00
Cut back-yard grass ($10.00)						√		$10.00
								$23.75

Shawn checked off each task as soon as she finished them each day and loved how completing each chore meant she would receive more money at the end of the week. She recently said, "I always looked at the grass and wished it would grow faster so I could cut it again **and make more money**. Grow faster!" As a young teenager, she started her own business mowing lawns: $5.00 for the front yard; $10.00 for the back yard.

No one had to remind Shawn to do these chores. And she was learning an important life lesson: *doing more gets you more.*

Include Your Kids In "Businesslike" Activities

In her book, *There's No Place Like (Working from) Home,* Elaine Quinn suggests:

1. Create a spot for the children reserved for those times when you're on the phone and need them to be quiet. Stock it with favorite snacks, toys, activity books, and puzzles.

2. Take your children with you when you go to buy office supplies or run other business-related errands [to make them part of your work tasks].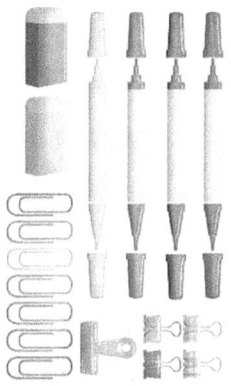

3. Set up a part of your office as their "office." Find tasks they can do, have them keep track of their work, and pay them. They'll love being part of your business!

4. Hold family "study hall" hours in the evening. Instead of fighting the children's needs for attention and inclusion, synchronize their needs with yours.

You Get What You Expect

In her book *Working from Home,* author Karen Mangia shares comments from the Moore parents about spending more of their working time at home with their two daughters.

"At first, the girls would come in every 15 to 20 minutes. Now we say, 'You can talk to Momma and Daddy at these times, but until then, get as much figured out on your own as you can.'

"[Daughter] Elizabeth wanted to work on the couch wrapped in a blanket with the dog on her lap. [Dad] Jack said, 'I wanted her to work from the table. But you pick your battles, right? I told her she could work from the couch only if she got a 90 or higher on her assignment.'

"When she turned in a 100, Jack rethought the idea of micro-management. He realized Elizabeth is a skilled negotiator. Maybe being comfortable is smart? That's true for kids, just like it is for adults.

"Their daughters became resourceful and self-monitoring, surprising both parents. 'Have we been underestimating ourselves and our kids all this time?' they asked themselves.

"They did it for the same reasons you and I work: ultimately, they wanted to get out and play. The girls did what they **needed** *to do so they could do what they* **wanted** *to do. That doesn't sound like child's play to me. That sounds like a valuable life lesson for all of us. Turns out we're all capable of more than we thought possible."*

Crowning Glory

As a teacher of fourth graders, Bunny Goar had a special rule during small group instruction: the children were not allowed to ask questions of her. She put a tiara on her head and told them, "When I'm wearing this tiara, you cannot talk to me." When a child inevitably broke the rule and came to her with a question, she pointed to her tiara, smiled, and shook her  head. Brilliantly, Mrs. Goar, the teacher, found a fun and sparkling visual cue. As a working-at-home parent, you might use a visual technique like Mrs. Goar's to signal, "You work independently while I'm working." (Or even adults? Ha ha.)

Maybe a goofy hat or flowery lei? Anything you say, Your Majesty.

 **TIP**   Expect more from your children.
They will surprise you.

29. Guard Your Time Like It's All You've Got. It Is!

J anis writes: I love writing this chapter. I confess that in controlling my own time, I'm the Wicked Witch of the West.

Some people (friends or neighbors, perhaps) assume that people who work from home have lots of free time and flexibility, and have trouble respecting "work time." It's just too easy to call or even drop in.

In the preface of my book on time management, *Manage Your Time Like It's All You've Got*, I wrote, *"I protect my time like a mama bear protecting her cubs. That means full-time vigilance* [and a guttural growl] *for intruders and a willingness to act."*

People who have been around me for a while know this because they see TIME- GUARDING behaviors. (Some of these people are even still my friends):

ABRUPT DEPARTURES*

1. **Leaving a room** to get back to my work area, even when "drop-in" visitors are present. I would never do this when I've invited people over. But if it's during my workday, drop-ins can also drop-out.

2. **Excusing myself** from my walking group after 45 minutes to get back to my project with only, "See y'all." No explanation or apology needed. Explanations just tempt people to respond, perhaps trying to persuade you to stay, or tell you how busy they are. In other words, explanations prolong the leave-taking and defeat your purpose.

3. **Traveling in my own car** rather than carpooling. Controlling the amount of time I spend at events is more important to me than saving gas or even enjoying the company of people I like while en route. If I were riding with someone else, it would be much more difficult to say, "I'm ready to leave now."

Abrupt departures: like when Supergirl slips away to save the planet, I slip away to save my time.

4. **Declining invitations** without a "good" reason. Not because something else is on my calendar. Just because I'd rather be doing something else. "I'll pass this time, but I know you'll enjoy it. Email me about how it went." Sometimes I can even say, "Please send me a photo." Notice I didn't say, "Call and tell me all about it." If I'm truly interested, I can enjoy skimming an email or looking at a

picture at the time of my choosing. Phone calls are trickier for a person as stingy with time as I am.

How do I get by with these "rude" habits in polite society?

1. When I've made plans to spend time with someone, work or personal, I give that time exclusively to that person or people. If meeting them in a public place, I leave my cell on until I "see the whites of their eyes," (until I know they aren't trying to get in touch). I turn the phone off as we approach each other and leave it off until we've said goodbye. As stated earlier, that's why God invented voicemail.

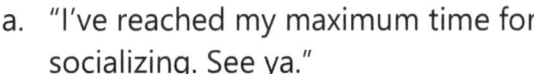

2. I poke fun at myself to let others know I'm the one with the weird personality; not them.
   a. "I've reached my maximum time for socializing. See ya."
   b. "Time for my introvert recharge. Bye!"
   c. "It's past my bedtime." (Might be at 5:00 in the afternoon.)

3. The longer I continue to do these things consistently, year-after-year, to guard my time, the more accepting and used to them people become: "She always leaves early. Nothing new."

4. If some folks do write me off as the Wicked Witch, I accept. It's like when Dolly Parton said, "The tabloids can't write anything bad about me. I've already told it all."

If we waste money, we can make more of it. Not so with time. Once it's gone, it's gone. It's literally priceless, so be choosy about giving it away.

Do It Just Because "They" Say So

Gail writes: My dad constantly used the phrase, "They say . . ." followed by sage advice and/or dire warnings. One day, after I was grown, he repeated the phrase and I said, "Dad, you've been referring to 'they' all my life. Who exactly is 'they'?" He paused for a minute, then said, "Well, actually, it's me."

TIP Give your time like you write checks. Be stingy.

How We Used the Tips in this Book to Write this Book

1.   We made our **workflow visible**. Above is our storyboard-on-a-rug. After we brainstormed the topics for this book, we printed each on brightly colored card stock and laid them out in no particular order. Like a giant jigsaw puzzle, we filled in the missing pieces.

2.   More card stock and a Sharpie (favorite **office supplies**!) were placed close by for all the changes and additions we knew we'd be making.

3.   We picked topics and began writing the first draft **(sub-goal)** of chapters at random. We placed the printed pages on each chapter title card as we completed them. All our chapters were created in a Dropbox shared file.

4.   We often read our chapters or paragraphs to each other aloud, on the phone or in person. We sometimes received compliments and sometimes even howls of laughter when our stories tickled our co-authors' funny bones. Doing this, we gave each other what we call **Proud Time**, which included the following:

   a. The pleasure of hearing our words immortalized by having another Human Being read them out loud

   Tell your colleagues and boss what you like about how they work with you.

   b. Pride and satisfaction as we listened to the favorable reviews from our respected co-authors

   c. Tip: be sure to give **specific, immediate, positive reinforcement** like this to your co-workers, team members, and even your boss (!!). This will keep them motivated and they'll be more likely to keep up with your excellent creativity and pace (see chapter 18).

5. **Positive reinforcement** from a respected colleague is a wonderful thing. It kept us writing and writing and writing, as we looked forward to seeing (and hearing) those pages being spit out of the printer (**feedback**).

6. We edited each other's chapters and printed our new "improved" versions. Then we each, at different times, sneaked into the storyboard room in the dark of night and replaced our co-author's "inferior" text with our "superior" text (always busted the next morning, though). Bad, bad. (Not a tip.)

7. Six times a day, Janis counted up the number of chapters written versus the number of orphan cards with no chapters completed (hoping the number would magically improve without her doing any work). This is called **procrastinating**. Oops, example of what *not* to do.

8. Mike sketched out three sections for the book and made large signs (**visual project management)** written with a thick marking pen. Very logical. Janis rearranged the chapters into their appropriate sections.

9. Happily for Mike and Janis, Gail agreed to become a co-author (**recruit talent and expertise**). She contributed stories that made us howl with laughter and jump with excitement at how perfectly her stories made serious points that readers will remember forever. (You'll thank us forever!) P.S. That's Gail you see leaping tall stacks of manuscripts in chapter 17.

10. We asked business owners to give us brutal **feedback** on our initial chapter ideas and cover designs. They took "brutal" seriously. Ouch. But priceless. As a result, we made major modifications to create the excellent beta-tested book you're reading now.

11. During the 3rd draft editing the co-authors each **let go** of some of our favorite ideas, stories, and words when other authors "made the case" that other choices might be better.

12. All these things together make for successful, productive, and fun time Working from Home. It's our SuperPower . . . and now it's yours!

FAQs

1. **What should I eat when working from home?**

   IT consultant Jack Joyner writes, "I confess I have eaten many bowls of cold cereal while staring at the barrage of incoming emails and deciding which to respond to first. Hint: Unsweetened spoon-sized shredded wheat lasts a long time in milk."

2. **What should I wear to work?**

   Business owner Michel Robertson says, "Quit work at 5 PM, at which time, change into a different pair of pajamas."

3. **I'm constantly getting annoying marketing calls at home when I'm trying to work. I feel guilty if I don't buy their product or send money to their organization. What should I do?**

   Send us your phone number.

4. **My heating bills have gone up now that I work from home all the time. Help!**

   Get a wood-burning stove. Test that it burns paper OK. Then send 1 cent to every letter you receive asking for money. Soon your mail carrier will deliver all the fuel you need every day for free.

Share Your Tips & Tribulations

We invite you to share your bloopers, blunders, or success stories about working from home by sending to janisallen@janisallen.com.

For information on corporate and volume discounts, please email
janisallen@janisallen.com

About the Authors

This is Gail's and Janis' second time to co-author a book. The first was *I Saw What You Did & I Know Who You Are,* published in 1990. Gail edited Janis' book *From Boo-Hiss to Bravo in 2020,* and at this writing, is editing her *Manage Your Time Like It's All You've Got.* The two also traveled together to Janis' client locations where Gail interviewed the managers and supervisors about their performance management success stories. Gail then wrote and published articles about their successes.

Mike and Gail were both Editor in Chief and writers for *Performance Management Magazine* (but not at the same time). Gail copy-edited Mike's book, *Sustain Your Gains.* So, you see, the three of us have a long, happy history with words and writing on business topics.

Gail co-authored the book *Removing Obstacles to Safety* with Dr. Judy Agnew in 2008. She has edited both fiction and non-fiction books. Gail holds a master's in communications, and as a freelancer, she will write and/or edit just about any subject (with some limitations). She has operated her own freelance business from home since 2004. Gail (whose coffee mug is at right) is married to Jack Snyder, who is a retired senior product engineer.  They have a son, David (Air Force Captain), daughter-in-law, Heather (fantastic Mom), and grandson, Knox (cutest kid on Earth, of course).

Gail spends so much time examining grammar, punctuation, formatting, and fonts that her sleep is invaded by same. In fact, she recently had a dream that she told someone to "Go to Helvetica!"

> **Gail dreamed that she told someone to "Go to Helvetica!"**

Mike and Janis are married business partners who work from home. They are writers, corporate trainers, curriculum designers and consultants, so they do similar things for a living. Mike's specialty is Lean and process improvement; Janis loves leadership and communication. Their daughter Shawn is a professor of English at Sungkyunkwan University in Seoul, South Korea.

Janis and Mike say, "The good news is that we can edit each other's work. The bad news is that we can edit each other's work." This book is our fourth co-authoring experience."

Gail began reading early as a child because she was often relegated to the sofa with bouts of bronchitis and pneumonia. There she often amused herself with reading, even while the rest of the family slept. As she grew up, she became interested in sports despite the health struggles and played on many interscholastic teams. She was a pitcher (for fast-pitch softball) for 10 years. She continues to read as much as possible, whenever possible and her first—maybe only—moment of daily Zen is that first cup of coffee while reading a book of choice.

Mike has been an avid reader since the third grade. He was one of those flashlight-under-the-covers readers after bedtime. He began collecting Marvel and DC Superhero comics when he was in college. Like millions of guys,

Mike read under the covers with a flashlight.

he laments the fortune lost in early Superman and Batman comics that his mother threw away. C'est un tragedie!

Janis read funnybooks at the washerette.

At eight years old, Janis could hardly wait to go with her mother to the washerette because the newsstand was right up the street. While her mother minded the washing and drying, Janis was buried in *Archie* and *Katy Keene*.

From navigating the written word to navigating the perils of working from home, we, like you, continue to meet these challenges with humor. May these SuperPowers be with you!

Janis Allen

Michael McCarthy

Gail Snyder

Recommended Resources

Presentations, Training and Online Courses

Want a presentation or training for your group based on this book? Ask us! Janis, Mike and Gail can be part of your "Talent and Expertise" team (Chapter 17, page 112) for projects, consulting, corporate meetings, conference presentations, publications, curriculum design, training and courses delivered online. Mike even delivered a Zoom workshop to a conference in Italy.

- For communications and leadership topics, go to www.JanisAllen.com
- For process improvement, Lean, performance improvement and safety topics, go to Mike at www.SustainLeanGains.com
- For editing of fiction, non-fiction and business materials, go to Gail at dgail01@bellsouth.net
- For book cover graphics and illustrations, go to Kathy Peterson at Adplus@mac.com
- For many of the books listed here, go to www.workingremotely.us

Books

1. *I Saw What You Did & I Know Who You Are: Bloopers, Blunders, and Success Stories in Giving and Receiving Recognition*, Janis Allen and Gail Snyder, Performance Management Publications, 1990, ISBN 0-937100-04-8

2. *Secrets of the Remote Workforce: By Employees. For Employees.* by Teresa Douglas, Holly Gordon, and Mike Webber, 750 Publishing, 2018, ASIN B07H7224XD

3. *Sustain Your Gains: The People Side of Lean-Six Sigma,* Michael McCarthy, Performance Management Publications, 2011, ISBN 978-0-937-100-20-2

4. *Professional in Pajamas: 101 Tips for Working from Home,* by Karen Adamedes, Abney Hall Pty Ltd., 2020, ISBN 978-0-9806364-3-7

5. *Death by Meeting* by Patrick Lencioni, Jossey-Bass, 2004, ISBN 0-7879-6805-6

6. *You Made My Day: Creating Co-Worker Recognition & Relationships,* by Janis Allen and Michael McCarthy, Performance Leadership Publications, 2005, ISBN 0-86730-787-0

7. *Manage Your Time Like It's All You've Got*, by Janis Allen, Shauna Costello, and Allison King, 2021, Key Press

8. *There's No Place Like (Working from) Home: Get Organized, Stay Motivated, Get Things Done*, by Elaine Quinn, Calloran Publishing, 2011, ISBN 978-0-9833235-3-2

9. *Don't Reply All: 18 Email Tactics That Help You Write Better Emails and Improve Communication with Your Team*, by Hassan Osman, Greenleaf Books, 2018, ASIN B018MGHZWO

10. *Work from Home Hacks: 500+ Easy Ways to Get Organized, Stay Productive, and Maintain a Work-Life Balance*, by Aja Frost, Adams Media, 2020, ISBN 978-1-5072-1559-3

Deck of Flash Cards

Winning Ways to a Positive Culture (deck of 52 playing cards with concrete ideas for co-workers and teams), by Janis Allen, Performance Leadership Publications, 2012, janisallen@janisallen.com $15.00

Videos

1. "Behavioral Techniques for Managing Your Time," by Janis Allen, 2021, ABA Technologies, www.abatechnologies.com

2. "Communication Can Make or Break Your Day" (30 minutes), Janis Allen and Michael McCarthy, 2006, Performance Leadership Publications, janisallen@janisallen.com $45.00

Audio

"Dos & Don'ts for Delivering Positive Recognition," by Janis Allen with Michael McCarthy, 2003, Performance Leadership Publications, www.janisallen.com

For information on corporate and volume discounts, please email
janisallen@janisallen.com

INDEX

5S (Five-S), 5, 6, 23, 56

Allen, David, 94
Army, United States, 148

Covey, Stephen, 88, 148, 167,

deadline, 33, 37, 38, 41-47, 49, 62, 90, 94, 101, 118, 121, 155, 163, 171, 172, 178
Deal, Let's Make a, 89, 109, 114, 124
decisions, 49, 53, 78, 92
declutter, 23
deskercise, 139
dishes, dirty, 31, 32, 35, 162
Distracto, Dr., 50, 94, 96, 163

email, xiv, 50, 56-58, 61-69, 71, 72, 74, 75, 82, 83, 94, 95, 100, 101, 107, 120, 121, 138, 190, 191, 197, 199, 206, 207
exercise, 73, 100, 133-139, 144

finish line, 45, 47

Goar, Bunny, 187
Good for Me chart, 183, 184
Groove, Greasing the, 137

hacks, 39, 139, 206
Halmshaw, Harry, ix, 136
Helprin, Mark, 178
homework, 165-167, 173, 184

interrupt, xv, 50, 53, 67, 75, 99, 101, 149, 162-164, 166, 167, 169-173, 175

Jackson, Stephen, ix, 66, 150
Joyner, Jack, ix, 123, 139, 197
Justice, Russell, ix, 79

kids, xv, 25, 52, 156, 182, 183, 185, 186

Lencioni, Patrick, 77, 205
Ludwig, Lori, ix, xv

Maag, Greg, ix, xiv
Mangia, Karen, 186
McCarthy, Shawn, x, 57, 67, 123, 137, 184, 185, 202
McKenzie, Kristen, 174
meetings, xv, 21, 51, 53, 77-80, 83, 84, 100, 118, 120, 121, 122, 134, 138, 147

naps, power, xix, 11, 126, 144, 147-151
No, Dr., 67, 164, 167, 177

Osman, Hassan, 61, 206
outsource, 109, 112, 113

Paige, Satchel, 142

pajamas, xix, 18, 81, 82, 95, 121, 147, 150, 173, 197, 205

Parton, Dolly, 191

passport, 12, 18, 16, 161, 164-166

Pausch, Professor Randy, 72, 73, 78, 93, 105

Peterson, Kathy, x, 15, 63, 66, 139

phone, xviii, 4, 6, 51, 53, 56, 67, 71-76, 83, 93, 100, 101, 110, 111, 120, 124, 134, 138, 141, 144, 149, 156, 158, 162, 185, 191, 194, 197

Premack, David, 90

ProcrastiNapper, 148

Procrastinasty, Dr., 45, 87, 89, 94, 96

procrastinate, 11, 18, 43, 49, 87, 90, 91

Rasheed, Eric, x, 129

re-direct, 170-172, 174, 175

response cost, 5, 164, 166

Robertson, Michel, x, 26, 114, 138, 177, 197

signs, 9-13, 16, 40, 81, 149, 158, 164, 195

Skinner, B.F., 5

sleep, xviii, 19, 44, 45, 61, 97, 143-145, 147-151, 202

Smith, Brenda, x, 39, 121, 124, 138

Snyder, David, 156, 181, 201

storyboard, 193, 195

water-cooler, 123, 124, 126

Wicked Witch of the West, 189, 191

workspace, xv, xix, xxi, 1, 3-5, 7, 9-12, 15-19, 23, 27, 95, 153, 162-166, 171, 176

Zoom, xix, 6, 80-82, 95, 123, 136
Zoom, Dr., 80, 81

Epilogue

Janis writes: Making the index was the hardest part of this book. I told Mike, "I'm never writing another book . . . and it won't have an index!"